BEN KEHOE

Innovation in Australia

Creating prosperity for future generations

Published by Ben Kehoe

1st Edition 2019, pbk.
2nd Edition 2020, pbk

ISBN: 978-1-925999-22-8 (print)
9781925999235 (epub)
9781925999242 (mobi)

Also available as an ebook from major ebook vendors

Reviews

This book is born of more than 35 years' experience working with organisations that want to do better and to be better. It is unashamedly a practitioner's view - a view from the Australian business trenches, with a focus on what we can and should do to enhance business and elevate national prosperity.

Kehoe's is a critical eye. He points to the lessons we have not learned about transformation and change in our approach to business and growing prosperity and worries about the future if these lessons remain unlearned.

As he says, in Australia we have a focus on sport and a Commission to help drive our success there; what about a Prosperity Commission? The Productivity Commission has a role to play, but he urges the development of a Prosperity Commission with independence from Government that has a broad ranging brief to identify what is required to create growth and prosperity in a disrupted economic era.

Throughout Kehoe's work there are gems of insight and opinion, challenge and an invitation to readers to engage in the debate about how we can all do better and be better - as business, government and as a nation.

This is a worthwhile read for anyone interested in business and prosperity, and particularly insightful for practitioners who will receive a glimpse of what a successful career assisting others with organisational transformation and change looks like and what such work can achieve.

Professor Sandra Harding AO, Vice Chancellor and President
James Cook University, Australia - Singapore

Ben Kehoe's book *Innovation in Australia: Creating Prosperity for Future Generations* is a great read. In fact, it is the first book I have read on Australian Innovation. Australia is competing globally, and we need an environment nurtured by all levels of government to position us as a continuing serious player. The alternative option does not bear thinking about.

Ben has in simple terms named many of the challenges and problems with the Australian business culture. What Australia needs is leaders (business and political) with foresight and guts – not leaders looking for a comfortable ride sponsored by someone else.

Politicians and business leaders need to nurture a purpose and passion for the Australian nation rather than spending time on doing deals with mates and bagging each other.

He proposes a number of ideas worth considering including a Prosperity Commission to extend our thinking about the future and a genuine bipartisan National Infrastructure strategy with major multigenerational initiatives announced each election term. It's a good read. I commend it to you.

John Wagner, Chairman, Wagner Corporation
(Builder of the first major airport in Australia in 50 years)

The time is now!

COVID-19 changed the world in ways no one planned or even anticipated. Australia had been cruising along in a bubble of economic growth and complacency which defied logic. We announced (mostly to ourselves) how clever we were! Our twenty-nine years of economic growth was unprecedented. It was a record. No one else had ever done it. Look, no hands!

During the mid-1990s, then Prime Minister John Howard said it was his vision for Australians to feel "comfortable and relaxed" about our past, present and future.[1] We know that economic systems move in cycles – it was only a matter of time before the bubble burst, but no one wanted to talk about it, much less have any national conversation about the future. It seemed beyond us.

When Malcolm Turnbull initiated the conversation about innovation two decades after Howard declared his vision, I had high hopes that finally we had a PM who would grasp the opportunities with both hands. Just maybe we would get our act together and address Australia's future. What a disappointment. The fanfare around innovation quickly faded away. One conclusion was that the innovation topic did not "resonate" with the average Australian.

It wasn't a surprise. Innovation in a vacuum means nothing. There was no context.

We were presented with an opportunistic set of policies designed around the current system. There were no great aspirations – or 'moon shots' as I refer to them in this book.

In a book called *Great Australian Speeches*, the editor suggests:

"Australians are famously distrustful of flowery phrases and unnecessary verbosity, preferring instead a language that is lean, direct and to the point - ***probably a reflection of a people historically more preoccupied with staying alive*** *than comfortably developing mission or vision statements."*[2]

1 https://www.youtube.com/watch?v=YA8yB9dqtJQ
2 https://www.goodreads.com/book/show/9810252-great-australian-speeches

Maybe it's a recipe for mediocrity?

COVID-19: a massive shift

The record of economic growth which we so proudly and frequently announced is over. Lockdowns, border closures, social distancing and a range of other precautions are part of our language and behaviour. Not only that, our need for information created an unhealthy dependence on the media. Feelings of community uncertainty, desperation and fear were palpable.

COVID-19 is the catalyst for change that no-one wanted or predicted. Its scale and impact are beyond comprehension. The world and Australia will never be the same. It will be with us for a while and we have to learn to live with it.

The very essence of our lives and many of the structures that we know, and love are changing. To name a few:

- Lives are now more transparently at risk – predominantly the aged (over 60) and those with comorbidities.
- The uptake of technology has accelerated – cashless transactions, Zoom meetings and working from home.
- Our relationship with work has changed – in some cases jobs are at risk.
- Businesses are fighting to survive (or are not surviving).
- The way we relate to our family, friends and colleagues is changing.
- Our way of life – the freedoms we took for granted, have been affected.

We are in a liminal moment – a time between times. We know that profound learning comes in times of great crises. How do we use COVID-19 as a time of deep learning? Words like 'reset', 'reshape' and 'revitalise' slip off the tongue. These words are similar to 'restructuring' and 'reform' which were used when the Australian economy was changing in the late 1980s and early 1990s. Globalisation was the catalyst back then.

It is a period we look back on as being momentous for our country. There was so much change back then, we even discussed the concept of 'change fatigue'. However it laid the platform for the nearly three decades of unbroken economic growth that followed. Economic restructuring. Microeconomic reform. Australia opened itself to the world. While globalisation was the catalyst, the Accord was a major process step to engage the stakeholders. It was a social innovation of the time. Business, unions and the government came together and worked together:

- floating the $,
- tariffs removed,
- banking deregulated,
- awards restructured,
- enterprise bargaining,
- the recession we had to have!

The pursuit of global competitiveness was a 'moon shot' for Australia – world class manufacturing was one aspiration with total quality management, value-added management, multi-skilling and training as tools. Management consultants with packages, programs and a plethora of management tools were everywhere. So, what happened?

A summary:

- 29 years of economic growth helped by massive Chinese demand for our resources.
- Australia is the richest country in the world (in terms of assets per capita).
- our manufacturing base continued its decline.
- we became a service economy.
- union membership declined dramatically.

We are proud of the result. We are good at talking it up! BUT?

Somewhere in there, the dream about global competitiveness evaporated – globalisation prevailed, and a maniacal pursuit of lower costs and efficiency drove decision-making. We transitioned to a service economy – when was that decision made?

While Australia has prospered over the past three decades, there has also been a cost. Our manufacturing sector has dramatically declined to less than 6% of GDP while other countries (including China, Japan and South Korea) have significantly increased their manufacturing capacity. We have become dependent on global supply chains.

A startling new report has revealed that Australia now ranks last among developed nations in terms of manufacturing self-sufficiency.[3] In fact, our global country ranking for manufacturing as a percentage of GDP is 103. We rank with countries like Samoa and Panama.[4] This decline has significant implications for our national security and resilience.

As this book goes to press the federal government has announced a major initiative to address Australia's manufacturing issues: The Modern Manufacturing Initiative.[5] Funding of $1.3 billion will be made available over the next four years in six national manufacturing priority areas:

- resources technology and critical minerals processing
- food and beverage
- medical products
- recycling and clean energy
- defence
- space

Industry will be engaged to co-design two, five and ten-year road maps in each of these priority sectors, setting goals that will guide the funding allocation.

These are early positive steps towards capitalising on the opportunity for Australia to innovate and become an advanced manufacturing hub – but do we have the will to make it happen? It is a long road back. To develop a low-cost, high-tech manufacturing capacity is a 30 to 50-year journey. I discuss this opportunity further in Chapter 6 of this book.

In addition to our manufacturing self-sufficiency issue:

- Australia is geographically located in the Pacific, far away from our cultural roots. We are culturally as well as geographically isolated. We are an 'Eurasian' nation.
- we are a democracy in a region where both the concept and practice of democracy frequently differs quite substantially from our view.

3 https://www.defenceconnect.com.au/key-enablers/6557-falling-well-behind-the-curve-australia-ranks-last-in-global-self-sufficiency-ranking
4 https://www.theglobaleconomy.com/rankings/Share_of_manufacturing/
5 https://www.industry.gov.au/news-media/modern-manufacturing-initiative-and-national-manufacturing-priorities-announced

- Australia is self-sufficient in many resources, but not in petroleum products. They come from the Middle East via Singapore and the South China Sea to South Korea. Their petroleum is refined before finished petroleum products are shipped to Australia. We are heavily dependent on offshore oil and hold only a 30-60-day fuel stock due to limited storage capacity.
- the sovereignty of The South China Sea is currently hotly disputed by several nations. In this context, Australia is vulnerable to political upheaval in the region. There is an obvious short-term solution: refine our petroleum in India or buy finished petroleum products from them. Coal is also a potential source of petrol.[6]
- Australia has no substantive shipping industry, which means our dependence on imports is at risk.
- many Australian industries are dependent on China. It is the source of many of our chemicals, spare parts and some manufactured technologies. We also have a very heavy pharmaceutical reliance on China. It provides over 90% of our pharmaceuticals.[7]

Only now (amid a tectonic shift caused by COVID-19) are some of these issues and their implications surfacing. I have heard little about them in my 50 adult years. Not having previously had these issues firmly on our national agenda is a form of strategic incompetence (or to put it bluntly, ignorance)!

National sovereignty (even smart sovereignty) is now an agenda for Australia. What does that mean? Who can articulate a narrative around it that ordinary Australians can buy into?

We are at the edge of a cliff and COVID-19 has brought us there faster than we ever could have anticipated – the opportunity to create a leading-edge 22nd century country is here now. Will we grab it with both hands?

As a nation, we are pretty good at 'pumping up our tyres' – we 'punch above our weight' is the message. In what I ask? Mining? Medical research? As you will discover in this book, in many global indices we are mediocre (in my view) for a country with the potential we have.

6 https://www.sciencedirect.com/topics/engineering/fischer-tropsch-process
7 https://www.afr.com/politics/federal/australia-dangerously-dependent-on-medical-imports-20200217-p541ej

Will Australia ever lead the world as an innovative nation?

In Chapter 1, I mention the establishment of the National Brand Advisory Council in 2019 "to oversee the development of a unifying national brand to help drive economic growth from international markets." Their national brand recommendations are now published. They include:

- a storytelling platform ("Only in Australia") to celebrate everything that's unique about Australia's people, place and product.
- visual brand design elements that include a wattle-inspired green and gold colour scheme and the use of the AU short-cut wording to also represent Australia.

However, at this stage the reception to the unifying national brand recommendations is underwhelming. They might take a while to get traction, if they ever do. Is this an example of our inability to accept innovation? The jury is out. Maybe a unifying national brand can be used as part of the leverage to position ourselves as the nation we need to become. A leader in Asia?

There have been many decisions in Australia's history that have influenced our business thinking. All of these decisions came from an elementary understanding of the importance of business in our world and a simplistic view that our raw materials were all we needed to be a wealthy country.

When we talk about Australia's performance, there is a mindset and language system in place which reflects a 20th century paradigm. GDP, debts and deficits, productivity, unemployment and inflation are all practical measures, but in many ways, they are limiting our conversation. Instead, we need to focus on building capability and prosperity for generations to come – i.e. for the 22nd century.

COVID-19 has changed many of the rules. A new paradigm is emerging. We can choose to be a part of creating this paradigm, or the world will do it for us. Being trapped in a 20th century mindset is no longer a safe option for Australians.

Loss of life, loss of livelihoods and loss of freedoms could just be the start – the prospect of living in this state of uncertainty is daunting. In a breath, the world is different. We are living in a liminal moment – much of what we knew and loved is gone forever, and the opportunity to recreate, revitalise and reset Australia for this new world is upon us.

Founding Singapore Prime Minister Lee Kuan Yew warned in 1980 that Australia risked becoming the "poor white trash of Asia"[8] if we didn't open up our economy. This phrase was repeated by Paul Keating in justifying the major economic reforms of the 1980s and 90s. It was confronting. The metaphor is still relevant today. The question now is whether our national narrative is robust enough to position us in the top 5 of the global indices I have nominated in the book. To ignore this question or to remain complacent leaves us in the risky position where we might in time be described as the "lifestyle trash of Asia".

We are now living in a world where the institutions which have sustained society for my lifetime and previous generations are under extraordinary pressure (including models of democracy and capitalism). Even the concept of leadership is taking a battering. Recent leadership in Australian business and politics has been egocentric (musical chairs), inward-looking (debts and deficits) and short term (election cycles). We can no longer afford this level of intellectual poverty.

The National COVID-19 Commission Advisory Board has been formed in the hope of creating a pathway to a new future. One can only hope we don't see yet another report – Australia is good at producing reports. We do them all the time. There have been close to 60 over the last 20 years on innovation and related topics alone!

The time is now: Australia has a choice.

There is mantra in the world of business that is worth pondering:

"If you always do what you have always done – you will always get what you have always got!" (Henry Ford) [9]

We need to create a new narrative for Australian business for the mid-to-late 21st century. It requires a mindset shift:

8 https://www.businessinsider.com.au/why-australia-is-in-danger-of-becoming-asias-digital-banana-republic-2015-10

9 https://www.goodreads.com/quotes/904186-if-you-always-do-what-you-ve-always-done-you-ll-always

20th Century	22nd Century
A mediocre business nation dependent on other countries for our economic survival	An Asian nation and a smart sovereign nation leading the world in creating global and national prosperity.
A nation of 'stonemasons'	A nation of 'cathedral builders'

If we stay the way we are now, we also run the risk of becoming one of the misguided disciples that de Mello referred to in his book, *The Song of the Bird.*

"When the guru sat down to worship each evening the ashram cat would get in the way and distract worshippers. So he ordered that the cat be tied during evening worship.

Long after the guru died the cat continued to be tied up during evening worship. And when the cat eventually died another cat was brought to the ashram so that it could be duly tied during evening worship.

Centuries later learned treatises were written by the guru's disciples on the essential role of the cat in all properly conducted worship."[10]

The messages in this book are even more relevant now than when I wrote them before the COVID-19 pandemic hit. Predictably, we're getting plenty of reports and government funding announcements. But what's missing is a series of mind-stretching national moon shots to challenge Australia and Australians to do and be better in the post-COVID-19 world. Industry has the opportunity to provide that leadership!

10 https://www.goodreads.com/book/show/345279.The_Song_of_the_Bird

Foreword

by EUAN MURDOCH
Founder and Managing Director Herron Pharmaceuticals

This is the first book I have read that confronts the issues around Australia's underperformance in the areas of innovation and commercialisation. Ben Kehoe earns the right to draw his worrying conclusion after more than 40 years working in the trenches as a "social technology" pioneer with over 250 CEOs in Australian business. In those 40 years there have been dramatic changes in the Australian business environment – he has worked with and guided CEOs as they have managed those changes. He has made a substantial difference in the businesses he has worked with and to the lives of the people in those businesses.

The environment now is even more challenging. Volatile, uncertain, complex and ambiguous is how it is described. Accelerating technology progress, artificial intelligence, the globalisation of markets, the emergence of sustainability, the green revolution and the rise of the Asian economic powerhouse led by China are just some of the challenges.

Australia has a well-deserved proud record for its many and varied inventions. However, our commercialisation record is poor. Many government reports attest to that fact. Looking to the future, we face some significant challenges.

More than 70% of our R&D expenditure occurs in university environments where there is a distinct lack of a commercial imperative, compared to 70+% invested by companies in R&D in other western nations. Australia's universities claim they have the competence to commercialise the Intellectual Property (IP) they generate, but by any measure, much of their IP either sits on the shelf or is spun out with sub-optimal outcomes.

In many of Australia's research institutions, there is a lack of trust between the scientific community and their commercialisation centres. In many cases, this is due to a poor understanding of where value is created along the commercialisation pathway. Most of the value creation from innovation occurs post the invention. Many of our scientists have an unrealistic view of what their share of the pie should be, and business has in many cases failed to argue their case, resulting in this lack of trust.

The reality is that we have a history of great Australian inventions BUT we are poor at commercialisation. The evidence is clear!

It is crucial for Australia to develop an entrepreneurial paradigm which measures R&D performance in terms of the number of 'for profit' businesses created. We need to have the frameworks and a language system in place to address prosperity and wealth creation, plus the associated financial systems and resources to allow our innovations to move from the lab to the consumer. When looking for our innovation commercialisation dollars (particularly for early stage IP), they are currently much more accessible offshore than domestically. Inevitably, in many cases this results in our IP ownership moving offshore.

Australia has a choice between contributing to (and being) a strong and vibrant part of Asia or being a second-class citizen. Ben asks the question: are we a 'settler' nation that is drifting to obscurity or are we up for the challenge of securing our future? It is a legitimate question.

With globalisation and the ever-increasing disruptive potential from inventions, the reality is that any new invention can have immediate global appeal. Australia's appetite for risk relative to other developed economies is low and many of our latest (and future) innovations are (or will be) snapped up by global players. Ben highlights the Gardasil story in this book as an example.

Ben consistently asks business leaders the tough business questions:

- what's your reason for existence?
- where are we going?
- what do we stand for (our values)?
- What is our highest aspiration?
- what difference are we making?
- what is our unique contribution?

These questions need to be asked in all businesses (and nations) today. He highlights the lack of vision and subsequent lack of dialogue about answering these fundamental questions in many of Australia's businesses and in government. At a national level, both our business and government leaders need to nurture these questions and the subsequent conversations.

By comparing Australia's fixation on our sporting success with our ambivalence when it comes to nation-building goals or moon shots, Ben highlights our lack of aspiration and dreams for building a greater Australia. Mediocrity is our standard!

For businesses to grow, prosper and contribute to Australia, they must work at reinventing themselves. It takes a level of competence not currently obvious in our national conversation. The key ingredients are imagination, foresight, courage, resilience, and as Ben says "some mongrel" to make the necessary hard decisions over a very long period of time. Individuals, companies and Australia have a choice to create their own futures, or have their futures determined by their competitors. (another company or another country.)

People (and countries) do not change their behaviour unless there is a crisis perceived or actual. Is there a crisis?

We owe it to future generations of Australians to embrace the learnings from Ben's book.

I wholeheartedly recommend *Innovation in Australia: Creating Prosperity for Future Generations*. This book should be compulsory reading for anyone interested (and concerned) about what the future holds for our children and grandchildren.

BEN KEHOE

Innovation in Australia

Creating prosperity for future generations

For my grandchildren:
Andrew, Jacob, Sam, Zack, Sebastian, Maya, Tobias, Sophia, Olivia, William, Genevieve, Annabelle and Edward.

Contents

Introduction

"The key to strategy is context."

—Stanley Davis[11]

Innovation emerged as a national agenda item when Malcolm Turnbull became Prime Minister in the musical chairs game we have played in Australia over the past decade with our most important leadership position.

That was only in 2015, even though it now seems like eons ago. At the time, I rediscovered a 1991 document in my files written by The Boston Consulting Group entitled *Innovation in Australia*. It was no surprise that it contained some of the same arguments which are current today. It kick-started this writing journey for me – discovering the innovation story in Australia.

Some 80 or 90 blogs and four years later I now have a book, *Innovation in Australia: Creating Prosperity for Future Generations*. It's been a fascinating journey. First the good news: I have discovered that Australia has a proud history of innovation extending back to the early 1800s. The bad news is that our record of commercialising these innovations and building wealth-creating industries is disappointing.

There have been multiple reviews of innovation (and related areas) in Australia over recent years. Our inability to commercialise innovations is an underlying theme in many of them.

Why is that?

Firstly, we're a country gifted with natural resources. We have made choices not to engage in creating wealth. For many reasons (not all of them obvious), we have opted to sell our raw materials offshore, leaving other countries to create the value.

Secondly, I believe the culture that has developed in Australia over time is centred on recreation and lifestyle.

And finally, there is no clear vision (or narrative) about Australia's future. This is obvious in our national conversations.

---

11 https://www.sciencedirect.com/science/article/pii/0090261682900365

This book is structured in four parts:

Part 1 – Our innovation story to date

Part 2 – Australia's current position

Part 3 – The challenges Australia faces in a rapidly globalising world.

Part 4 – A new Australian narrative for the future.

Part 4 focuses on the need for what I call 'vision-driven planning', so that future generations of Australians will be able to prosper into the 22nd century. We need to secure our place in the new global economy.

Vision-driven planning involves leaders from all sectors of the community coming together to formulate a shared vision (story) for the future. This vision provides a sense of shared direction.

Unfortunately, there is an absence of vision-driven planning in Australia. In my lifetime I remember very few vision-driven objectives or statements, and the major infrastructure projects we've attempted have been political footballs. With the rate of change accelerating, we are too comfortable. It reminds me of the 'boiling frog' analogy which I first heard in the economic restructuring debates of the 1980s.

The 'boiling frog' is a fable describing a frog being slowly boiled alive. The premise is that if a frog is put suddenly into boiling water, it will jump out, but if the frog is put in tepid water which is then brought to a boil slowly, it will not perceive the danger and will be cooked to death.

While this is not a true story – the message is clear.

Mt Everest is often used as a planning metaphor. A simple story: two mountain climbers are setting their goals – one stakes out Mt Kosciusko, and the second stakes out Mt Everest. The level of preparation, training, dedication and commitment required is profoundly different for each of those projects.

On a good day in Australia, we might discuss a local hill.

The 1961 vision about landing a man on the Moon announced by President Kennedy is one planning metaphor not often used in Australia. But it united a nation.[12] When that goal was achieved in 1969, it was a global moment. Most who were alive then vividly remember where they were when it happened. *"One small step for man one giant leap for mankind."*[13] I use the term 'moon shots' in this book as a metaphor for goals/intentions to which Australia could aspire.

I'm a management consultant. I've worked with Australian business and government on projects focusing on strategy development and change management for over 40 years. I dare to speculate that I was one of the very few in the early 1980s working with Australian businesses on strategy. It was such a novel concept. I can tell stories about business owners and CEOs who laughed when the concept of planning for any more than a year was proposed – "we have the budget, that's all we need" was the challenging response to any longer-term proposals. Many of those businesses no longer exist or they are owned by international investors.

In many ways I've contributed to innovation in Australia – sometimes directly, but mostly indirectly. My work has focused almost exclusively on strategy development and executing all of the changes which have ensued. For many businesses with whom I worked, it was the first time their boards/leadership teams had participated in strategy planning processes using group learning technologies. In the early 1980s, not only was strategy a 'new' concept but planning in teams was revolutionary. Having lived on the edge of social change for this whole time, I now have a much deeper grasp of the challenges and issues that face Australia as we are drawn into a change whirlpool more disruptive than we've ever seen.

I've written this book as a small contribution to the thinking on the need for innovation in Australia, based on working with more than 250 businesses over the last 40 years. I'm sure there are as many views on innovation as there are business leaders. I talk about where we are now, how we got here, and how we must create a new narrative for our future in a rapidly changing world.

The year 2050 is maybe just a bit far for me at 69, but my grandchildren will be in the prime of their lives.

12 https://er.jsc.nasa.gov/seh/ricetalk.htm
13 Astronaut Neil Armstrong's famous words when first setting foot on the Moon.

What will their world be like?

In which industries will they be building businesses?

Decisions made today in business and government will determine the answers to those questions. They need to be answered in this time window.

If you agree with the content of this book – great. Even better if you start contributing to the discussion.

If you think it's rubbish – eureka! You've read it and you're engaged with the topic.

I am interested to hear your view.

For those who have no view – you haven't read or thought about the issues we're facing. You probably view our challenges as someone else's problem. I recently heard the following observation about the settlement of Australia vs the US – "The convicts arrived sponsored by England and asked, 'What's for lunch?'."[14] The Government provided it, and nothing has changed. We still suffer from this dependence mentality and we are very critical when anything disrupts it.

Throughout this work I have provided many facts that were a revelation to me. I hope you can take the time to pause and reflect on them and to think about the possibilities for Australian business innovation.

I also hope that over time we can build a strategic conversation about some of the important issues I raise in this book.

14 https://www.abc.net.au/radio/programs/conversations/damien-cave-new-york-times/11197162

PART ONE

Our Innovation Story To Date

Chapter 1

AUSTRALIA'S INNOVATION HISTORY

"When we crow about products such as Vegemite, Victa lawnmowers, Hills Hoists and Speedo swimming costumes, we seem to feel some kind of ownership, not just over the pair in the second drawer at home, but over the entire product range."

—Matthew Richardson[15]

Introduction

The purpose of this chapter is to document a perspective on the early days of innovation in Australia. It provides a historical context which is an important part of understanding Australia's innovation journey.

For at least 60,000 years prior to our settlement, Australia's Indigenous people lived in this land. The British settlement of Australia was a form of social innovation/disruption and sadly there were/are many casualties. The current debate over Australia Day and the settlement or 'invasion' of Australia is an important part of our national story and over time reconciliation is an imperative.

How it will happen is a long way from being agreed or clear. There have been some small steps on this journey and the Uluru statement is another important step.[16] There must be a continuing dialogue and an openness of spirit which enables it to become an important part of any discussion on national prosperity.

Many years ago, my wife Sally and I attended a workshop with Jean Houston.[17] I have never forgotten one statement she made:

"When Australia finally reconciles with its Indigenous people and the great traditions of the land, it will have a special place in the world."

It's worth thinking about.

---

15 https://trove.nla.gov.au/work/9666598?q&versionId=11219873

16 https://www.aph.gov.au/About_Parliament/Parliamentary_Departments/Parliamentary_Library/pubs/rp/rp1617/Quick_Guides/UluruStatement

17 http://www.jeanhouston.com/

The Early Settler Economy

There are many elements to the story, and it's important to understand our significant founding steps.

- James Cook was the first British explorer to see Australia in 1770.
- Over the next few years, Britain decided they needed a new destination to send convicts. The US Revolutionary War precluded them being sent there. The British gaol system was overcrowded, so Britain invested in a project to relocate many unwanted prisoners to our shores.
- In 1788, New South Wales was settled at Port Jackson by Captain Arthur Phillip. The deliberate establishment of the first penal settlement in a new land. Another innovative step.
- Over the next 80 years, Britain established a number of penal settlements in the Australian colonies and transported more than 160,000 convicts here.[18] Many convicts were unwilling settlers who had committed what we now might see as very minor crimes. They were supervised by soldiers who were 'not elite'.
- Free settlers increasingly arrived during the penal colony period. Over time there were assisted migration programs. As it happens my ancestors arrived from Ireland in about 1860. Free settlers came in search of a better life. Sound familiar?
- In the 1850s/60s after gold was discovered, the different colonies emerged as more independent and fragmented. All colonies reported directly to England. It was not until the late 1800s that the colonies started to meet to explore issues of common interest and an emerging sense of an Australian identity began to form.
- Australia remained as a number of independent colonies until Federation in 1901. It took 113 years from the British settlement to forge a nation named Australia.

By 1913, the National Museum of Australia records that *"Australia enjoyed an international reputation as the social laboratory of the world. With high tariffs to keep out cheap goods, the 'White Australia' policy to keep*

18 https://www.nla.gov.au/research-guides/convicts

out cheap workers, and arbitration to establish industrial awards, invalid pensions, a minimum wage and an eight-hour day, Australia was called a 'working man's paradise' compared to other nations".[19]

The whole venture was an investment by Britain in a new land. A number of colonies were 'founded' and funded over a number of years. These colonies remained independent of each other but dependent on Britain until Federation and beyond.

Australians remained British citizens until 1949 until the Nationality and Citizenship Act was passed in 1948 and came into effect on 26th January 1949.[20] Britain remained a major trading partner for an extended period in the 20th century. Our Head of State (the Governor-General) is the representative of the Monarch of Australia, currently Queen Elizabeth II.

The establishment of penal colonies in the 'Great Southern Land' was a government-sponsored decision. I suspect it was more a problem-solving decision than any grand vision by the British government. Extending Britain's global reach was part of the plan but in my many years I have never heard it described as anything other than the establishment of penal colonies.

It is not my intention in this book to rewrite the history of Australia, but it is important to gain an understanding of how our 'early settler economy' started. Established businesses were non-existent when the colonies were founded. A grant of land was a common reward for new settlers and reformed convicts. Limited business activity was started by soldiers and freed convicts. Government was the source of much commercial activity instead, and with sealing and whaling as early exports and farming as a platform, our Australian business system evolved.

I believe that this very embryonic settlement of Australia and the subsequent business culture that emerged still influences how Australia sees itself as a business nation today.

19 https://www.nma.gov.au/exhibitions/glorious_days/about/a_social_laboratory?result_376675_result_page=2#slideshow-gallery

20 https://www.aph.gov.au/About_Parliament/Parliamentary_Departments/Parliamentary_Library/pubs/BN/0910/AustCitizenship

In today's business environment, the founding colonies might all have been considered 'start-ups'. It is only after each colony was up and running that the prospect of Federation became an issue and the formation of a nation became the agenda.

Australia continues today as an ongoing social innovation (not unlike a start-up business). In fact, there are many businesses/organisations in the world dating back to the 800s, long before the British settlement of Australia:[21]

- 803 – Stiftskeller St. Peter founded in Salzburg, Austria
- 1040 – Weihenstephan Brewery founded in Freising, Germany
- 1498 – The Shore Porters Society founded in Aberdeen, Scotland

There may soon be companies with a value that's worth more than the size of the Australian economy. For example, when Apple became the first company to be valued at $1 trillion in 2015, Australia's GDP was $1.58 trillion.[22]

The Lucky Country

Australia has basked in the 'lucky country' metaphor for decades. There is no shortage of references to this image. Donald Horne popularised it in publishing his book in 1964. He contextualised a country which had survived World War II, had stable government, abundant natural resources and a lifestyle which was incomprehensible anywhere else.

There is also an image so ingrained in our national psyche that it's taken for granted – we are 'the lifestyle country'. In other words, we tend to choose recreation above everything.

There is a genre of books using Donald Horne's classic metaphor as a theme, including:

- *When the Luck Runs Out: The Future for Australians at Work* (Fred Hilmer).[23]
- *The Lucky Country? Reinventing Australia* (Ian Lowe).[24]

21 https://www.businessinsider.com.au/oldest-companies-on-earth-2014-8?r=US&IR=T
22 https://www.smh.com.au/business/the-economy/apples-revenue-bite-could-soon-be-bigger-than-australia-20150428-1muxuw.html
23 https://www.amazon.com/When-Luck-Runs-Out-Australians/dp/006312064X
24 https://www.goodreads.com/book/show/28592620-the-lucky-country

- *The Lucky Culture* and the Rise of an Australian Ruling Class (Nick Cater).[25]
- *Australia 2034: Luckier by Design* (Nigel Andrade and Peter Munroe).[26]
- *Has the Luck Run Out? What We Can Do to Redefine Australia's Future* (David Fagan).[27]

The Lifestyle Country

If you take the time to review Australia's business history – it is impossible to miss the major industrial relations debates of this country – one issue stands out above all else: lifestyle/recreation. In fact, it seems as if all the major workplace debates in the country have been about major recreational advances. Here are a few examples.[28]

Year	Milestone
1920	The 44-hour working week is introduced.
1941	Annual leave of one week becomes standard.
1945	Annual leave of two weeks is introduced.
1948	The 40-hour working week is introduced.
1949	The 35-hour week and long service leave is introduced in the coal industry.
1963	Three weeks of annual leave becomes the standard.
1973	Four weeks of annual leave is introduced.
1981	The 38-hour working week is introduced.

25 https://www.goodreads.com/book/show/17899174-the-lucky-culture-and-the-rise-of-an-australian-ruling-class
26 https://www.goodreads.com/book/show/36106127-australia-2034?from_search=true
27 https://www.goodreads.com/book/show/44098624-has-the-luck-run-out
28 www.actu.org.au

In addition, there have been other recreational advances over the years, for example penalty rates and 17.5 % holiday leave loading. While all these conditions have created a wonderful lifestyle, there is a cost. Australia is a country of enormous potential, and in many ways, we are too comfortable – our lifestyle is paramount.

The Lifestyle Cost

I have heard said many times (cynically) that Australian business shuts down on Melbourne Cup Day and does not reopen until Australia Day. This statement is a wake-up call. Prawns on the barbie, beaches, bikinis and board shorts. The land of the long weekend – these images are tattooed on our national psyche.

In recent years, we have seen many Australian-owned businesses sold to foreign companies. Why do they see value that we are unable to realise?

Choose an industry in Australia and you'll find many of the businesses operating here are either partially or fully owned by international investors. And of course, our car manufacturing industry did not survive.

A story was forwarded to me after Toyota closed down. It was reported that a former senior executive said the following at a business group lunch after the closing of the company's Altona Plant in Melbourne in 2013.

> *Last year in 2012, we were working so hard to create conditions, whereby we could stay in this wonderful country, and produce cars.*
>
> *We had restructured the business, and despite acceding to recent union demands, for even better wages and conditions, we were seeing a dim light, flickering at the end of the tunnel.*
>
> *We were honest with our employees and had explained the seriousness of the company's plight.*
>
> *They had assured us of their cooperation, so we were determined to all pull together, in a desperate attempt, to keep the company viable.*
>
> *There was an air of camaraderie. A feeling of hope.*
>
> *It was Australia Day that week, and it fell on a Thursday.*

On the Friday, out of our workforce of 2418:

757 workers called in sick

568 workers just didn't turn up

431 workers were on holidays

662 workers turned up for work

That's when I finally realised, we were stuffed.[29]

It may well be an exaggerated story, but the message is clear that we are a country devoted to lifestyle. But we need to delve some more into Australia's history to understand our present-day business culture.

Defining Moments in Australian History

The National Museum of Australia has published a list of defining moments in Australia's history.[30] I perused their list of more than 150 defining moments and found that only about 30 are related to business or wealth creation. I divided those 30 moments into the three categories in the table on the next page.

29 http://pickeringpost.com/story/toyota-a-telling-tale-/2759
30 http://www.nma.gov.au/defining-moments/explore-defining-moments?from=0

	Emerging Business in Australia	Nation-Building Infrastructure	Industrial/Social Innovation
1797	Introduction of Merino sheep		
1851	Gold rushes in New South Wales and Victoria		
1854		Australia's first railway line opens in Victoria	
1856			Melbourne building workers win an 8-hour day
1872		Completion of the Overland Telegraph from Darwin to Port Augusta, South Australia	
1880	The Bulletin established in Sydney		
1885	Victorian Employers Union formed		
1885	BHP begins mining silver, lead and zinc in New South Wales		
1887	Chaffey Brothers introduce irrigation on the Murray River		
1901		Inauguration of Commonwealth of Australia	
1903	William Farrer begins distribution of Federation wheat		
1907			Justice Higgins hands down 'Harvester Judgement' (minimum wage)
1912			Maternity allowance introduced

	Emerging Business in Australia	Nation-Building Infrastructure	Industrial/Social Innovation
1913		Foundation of Canberra as the national capital	
1917		Completion of the Trans-Australian Railway linking Western Australia and the eastern States	
1920	QANTAS established		
1932		Foundation of the ABC	
1945	Penicillin developed		National introduction of employment and sickness benefits
1945		Post-War migration	
1948		Australia's first locally made car (the Holden 48-215) launched	
1949		Snowy Mountains Hydro-Electric Scheme launched	
1956	Television introduced for Australia's first Olympics		
1960	Restrictions on exports of iron were lifted		
1972			Equal pay for men and women
1978		SBS established	
1983	Floating the $A		
2004	Australia signs a free trade agreement with the US		

This exercise raised some interesting questions for me:

- what role does Australian business play in Australian society?
- should Australian business play a larger leadership role in establishing strategic directions for Australia?
- why isn't the founding of more Australian businesses listed?
- why aren't the sale of iconic Australian businesses listed?
- why aren't there more nation-building projects listed?

I also found it interesting that the Australian Agricultural Company (founded in 1824) is not listed and that the Sunshine Harvester Company is remembered for the 'Harvester Judgement' minimum wage case, and not for the fact that it was one of our first major manufacturing companies. It employed many Australians (and was sold in the 1950s to international interests).

Why is it that there are so few entrepreneurial businesses mentioned in the milestone moments recorded by our national museum? Is it that business is not valued by those who write our history? Or is business just not valued in Australia?

It might be argued that we are a small country and that a shortage of capital limited our capacity to build businesses over the long term. That has not stopped Israel or Singapore. Israel has the highest density of start-ups in the world (3,850 or one for every 1,844 Israelis). In addition, more Israeli companies are listed on the NASDAQ exchange than those from all European countries combined.[31]

We need to understand that Israel's determination has been driven by many things. Not the least of which being:

1. the threat of annihilation and
2. the fact they had little water (similar to us).

Is it any wonder they are driven?

31 *The Start-Up Nation: The Story of Israel's Economic Miracle*, Dan Senor and Saul Singer.

They faced an existential threat, being attacked at least twice by neighbouring countries that were intent on obliterating them. Their response has been to build a leading-edge defence system which enabled them to defend themselves. It has spawned a major technology industry. Many of the world's major technology companies now have R&D facilities in Israel, including Intel, IBM, Google, Facebook and Hewlett-Packard.

Israel also now leads the world in irrigation systems.

Only recently I read an article entitled *12 impossible ideas that Israelis turned into reality.*[32] They recently launched and landed their first space mission to the Moon – Australia was a leader in space research at one time.[33] Can anyone name any impossible projects we are working on in Australia?

But Israel as a country has only been in existence a relatively short time compared to Australia. Why are they more innovative?

Perhaps it's because our business culture is also committed to lifestyle and 'letting the government do it'. Australia is endowed with an abundance of natural resources.

Primary industry underwrote our early success. Sheep and wool were the basis of that success. There are anecdotes that when wool was exported to England, deliberate decisions were taken not to wash it because doing that was labour intensive and did not make economic sense. The wool was not processed in any way, it was just crudely compressed unwashed into bales complete with outback dirt and dust.[34]

Since then, decisions not to value-add in Australia have been the norm. Our abundant mineral resources have continued to deliver prosperity. Someone said to me recently (in the spirit of recreation) that "we surf the waves of commodity booms". There is no doubt we have developed a robust and stable business system, and we are generally very comfortable with our 'lifestyle'. We have experienced 28 years of economic growth to 2019. I guess the question going forward becomes – how do we sustain this wonderful existence? One former Australian Prime Minister compared

32 https://www.israel21c.org/12-impossible-ideas-that-israelis-turned-into-reality/
33 https://www.space.com/spacex-israeli-moon-lander-satellites-launch-success.html
34 https://www.goodreads.com/book/show/14891868-why-australia-prospered

living here as having won the lottery of life.[35] That's a great metaphor for the majority of Australians.

Recently, a National Brand Advisory Council of industry leaders was set up to help boost Australia's image overseas. The Council includes mining magnate Andrew Forrest, Australia Post Managing Director Christine Holgate, Qantas CEO Alan Joyce, Coopers Brewery chairman Glenn Cooper and Atlassian co-founder Mike Cannon-Brookes. The minutes of their first meeting highlighted some of the contradictions of Australia's history and culture that affect our ability to complete on the world stage.

"We think we are young, yet we have one of the oldest indigenous people and cultures; we love to win, but hate winners – we like the underdog, observe the tall-poppy syndrome;....

There's a certain resiliency and toughness around Australians that exhibits in many industries.... (But we) often seek external, overseas, validation before we achieve domestic recognition.... research shows Australia ranks well in physical beauty, enjoyability and lifestyle, but poorly on culture, innovation and technology... For better or worse, we have done an excellent job promoting our great physical and lifestyle attributes, while failing to translate other parts of our story to the world. Australians invented Wi-Fi, have some of the world's leading companies and brands, and our creative industries are highly influential and productive. We have a bigger story to tell and we need to get better at doing it."[36]

What is that story?

The statement in the minutes that we *"...have some of the world's leading companies and brands"* is surely hyperbole. QANTAS and?

So we get another report and a bundle of recommendations for $10 million.

35 https://www.news.com.au/national/nsw-act/prime-minister-tony-abbotts-speech-from-the-national-press-club-in-canberra-on-february-2/news-story/e978c62e44518d9613f132269973cad8

36 https://www.theaustralian.com.au/national-affairs/foreign-affairs/industry-leaders-to-overhaul-nations-overseas-image/news-story/f8aeeebc103be81cfe0c631a461c2eb7?from=htc_rss

Our DNA

I believe that starting innovative entrepreneurial businesses is simply not in our DNA. European settlement of Australia in 1788 created multiple British government-funded outposts for the first 70 or 80 years. We were a 'little brother/sister' in the new world.

But while the founding of Australia was ground-breaking, innovation was not front and centre. Our political and legal systems are effectively the British systems with some modifications – e.g. Federation. We actually swallowed the British legal and political systems whole. The formation of Australia via the Federation was a great achievement, but there was none of the soul-searching and anguish about the nature of our system that occurred in the United States. And maybe that is reflected in the stability and robustness of our system.

The potential downside is that stability and security are right at the heart of our culture. It is this stability which has allowed and encouraged immigrants from all parts of the world to settle and establish themselves in Australia. The Chinese in the 1800s, the southern Europeans in the mid-1900s, the Vietnamese in the 1970s, plus the more recent wave from the Middle East. Each of these cultural groupings has contributed uniquely to the Australian small business culture which exists today. Agriculture, hospitality, transport and construction are just some of the industries where the contribution of immigrants is obvious.

Nation-building projects focusing on physical infrastructure have been few and far between. The establishment of Canberra as our capital city is an outstanding exception. The Snowy Scheme is often touted as a great nation-building project. However, few others stand out.

When Australia was settled and for the next 100 years, there were two obvious 'competitive disadvantages':

1. there was limited water, and
2. we were geographically isolated.

We have done little to address these two issues since Federation and they have constrained us. For example, it is argued that the population of Australia is limited partially because of our lack of water. It remains a critical issue for us. Snowy 2.0 is one small step, but it is hardly nation-building.

Water is also used as an excuse for the way the population has settled. Our major population centres are in south-eastern Australia (Sydney, Melbourne and Brisbane), with outposts in Adelaide and Perth. There has been minimal effort in the last 50 years to decentralise development in Australia.

Australians are shocked to the core when cataclysmic floods occur and destroy homes and farmlands. And they occur regularly. But this shock quickly fades away when the trauma passes.

Australians also tend to be similarly shocked when we have extended periods of drought. There is much wailing and gnashing of teeth and outpourings of support for the victims, be they farmers or small rural communities. And governments promise more money as the solution. Each of these natural disasters is predictable and we like to congratulate ourselves on our compassion and generosity when they happen.

One possible solution is often promoted during times of flood and drought – the Bradfield Scheme for water diversion (first proposed in the 1930s for some of the water management issues in Australia). It re-emerges regularly as a conversation piece, but it is instantly dismissed as too hard or too expensive.[37] With the technology available today, it is reasonable to assume that water solutions are available. Yet we are so good at dismissing ideas. Apparently, the problem will be solved over time with more government relief.

Surely in the 21st century (nearly one hundred and twenty years since Federation) there have been many opportunities to address these major problems. But it is hard to remember when we last built a dam or water storage system of significance in Australia. People laugh when the idea of using the abundant water in the North of Australia as a solution to our drought problems is raised. Why is that? Lack of foresight? Fear? More self-interested priorities? A complacent attitude?

Water has always been an issue on the Australian continent. We learnt at school that Australia is the driest continent on the planet. Why then doesn't

37 https://www.queenslandcountrylife.com.au/story/5907676/bradfield-scheme-remains-a-dream/

Australia lead the world in water management (storage)? Is there nothing to learn from Israel?

In a world where 'impossible and expensive' projects are being proposed and completed in many countries – our solution is to dismiss the problem and expect the government to provide infinite funding to enable drought and flood recovery.

How much money has been spent on drought relief and flood relief over the past 50 -100 years? What if our engineers and scientists had real imagination and/or our political leaders had real foresight and courage? If not a technologically advanced version of the Bradfield Scheme, then what? In China there is a multi-decade project underway to solve their water problems which I'll talk more about later in this book.[38]

Australia also has more energy resources than almost any country in the world, why are we not leading the world in energy management? We don't seem to have the competence or the willingness to supply ourselves. Our energy system seems to have achieved third-world status.

Our geography has been used as an excuse for everything. Logistics is a major cost of doing business. Exporting from Australia is difficult and costly. We have an outstanding record of exporting raw materials and commodities, but little value-added product. That's too hard.

It took over 30 years for the Inland Rail (Melbourne to Brisbane) to get traction and that has only happened recently. So when is the rail to Darwin planned? In a world that's changing as rapidly as it is, this decision-making process is snail-like. How long has it taken to make a decision about the second Sydney airport? How long will it take to build?

The Wagner family in Toowoomba shattered the equilibrium when they opened an airport (privately built and owned) just outside Toowoomba at Wellcamp (140 kilometres west of Brisbane). It was built in 19 months and 11 days. Now fresh produce is delivered to Asia weekly. This is game-breaking stuff, especially in Australia when major decisions take forever. What a model for Australia.

38 https://thewest.com.au/business/construction/the-worlds-9-biggest-mega-projects-under-way-right-now-ng-b88772269z

The newly federated Australia gained an international reputation as having progressive social policies.[39] Many of these policies have worked well and provided a solid social platform for Australians, but have they come at the cost of fostering an innovative business culture? Consider this list:

Computers

Believe it or not, Australia was an early leader in computer research. CSIRAC (an acronym for Council for Scientific and Industrial Research Automatic Computer) was just the fifth stored program computer ever developed. And it was built in Australia in the late 1940s. It was fully operational by 1951, but that was the same year that a government decision was made to phase out computer research. The development of that type of technology was not seen as a priority for a resource-rich, commodities-exporting country like Australia.

Black Box Flight Recorder

And did you know that although Australian David Warren invented the first 'black box' flight recorder in 1954, the Department of Civil Aviation thought that it would be 'of little immediate use' because they had an excellent flight safety record. Six years later after an inquiry into a plane crash, the Australian government bought a flight recorder model that was technically inferior to Warren's invention.

Transistors

Another missed technology opportunity happened in the 1950s. The CSIRO was researching transistor technology, but when they asked for extra funding they were knocked back because there was an existing electronic valves industry in Australia. The transistor research was abandoned. Within five years, the entire electronic valve industry had been replaced by transistors that Australia then had to import from overseas.

Satellites and Space Research

In the 1960s, experimental satellites were being produced in South Australia and fired from Woomera. This program ended in 1971, and some of the

39 http://www.nma.gov.au/exhibitions/glorious_days/about/a_social_laboratory?result_376675_result_page=2

equipment was sold to Sweden. Now Sweden is a world leader in space research.

In recent years, the Government announced it was resurrecting our Space program.[40] The Australian Space Agency was established in 2018.

These decisions have been costly for Australia. Other countries have built industries that could have created wealth here. Why did we let major technologies like these go? Who knows, but some of the reasons surely included:

- lack of foresight
- lack of courage
- lack of competence, and/or
- fear.

There is another possibility – we have been and are complacent and comfortable. We have a relaxed, 'it will be right' attitude.

Australian Innovations that Changed the World

Australians have actually generated a lot of innovative ideas and products. Unfortunately, the average Australian has little knowledge of these achievements. Few Australians understand our innovation history. It is difficult to find businesses or industries which have their roots in Australian innovation. Innovation is not a dinner table conversation in Australian homes or a water-cooler topic in the workplace – sport of any kind, whining about the government and planning recreation take the lead.

In the Australian culture, much greater kudos is given if you know about Australian cricket captains over the years, or who won gold medals and football grand finals.

One only has to reflect on the Test cricket 'ball tampering' incident to see the impact of sport on our national psyche. There is very little kudos for knowing Nobel Prize winners or great Australian innovators or inventors.

40 https://australianaviation.com.au/2019/03/adelaide-getting-two-new-space-facilities/

The following table documents an aggregation of the Australian innovations that have changed the world.[41,42,43] Each of these innovations/inventions is significant, but it's interesting that very few have led to the development of major businesses/industries in Australia. Our excuse seems to be that we are poor at the process of commercialisation. I refer back to the story about our first exporting wool to England.

The Innovation	The Innovator	When
Transport		
Pre-paid postal system	Postmaster-General's Department (now Australia Post)	1838
Black box recorder	David Warren	1954
Seat belts	Monash University scientists	1964
Inflatable escape slide and raft	QANTAS	1965
Agriculture and Food		
Stump-jump plough	Richard Bowyer Smith	1875
Combine harvester	Hugh Mackay	1885
Wine casks	Tim Angove	1965
Tank-bred tuna system	Hagen Stehr	2008
Energy and Environment		
Permaculture	Bill Mollison	1972
Health		
Electronic pacemaker	Dr Mark Lidwell (Sydney Crown Women's Hospital)	1926
Medical application of penicillin	Professor Howard Florey	1939
Plastic spectacle lenses	Sola Optical	1960

41 http://www.australiangeographic.com.au/topics/history-culture/2010/06/australian-inventions-that-changed-the-world/

42 http://www.buzzfeed.com/vividsydney/australian-inventions-that-changed-the-world#.bcZ4a0x1B

43 http://the-scan.com/2015/12/05/9-surprising-australian-innovations-that-changed-the-world/

Health (continued)		
Ultrasound scanner	CSIRO	1976
Cochlear implant (bionic ear)	Dr Graeme Clark	1978
Continuous Positive Airway Pressure (CPAP) machine	Professor Colin Sullivan	1980
Spray-on skin	Dr Fiona Wood (Perth Hospital)	1991
Gardasil/Cervical cancer vaccines	Professor Ian Frazer	1991
Disease-diagnosing nano-patches	The University of Queensland	2014
Leisure		
Frazier lens	Jim Frazier	1998
Australian rules football	Tom Wills	1858
Box kite	Lawrence Hargrave	1893
Full-length feature film	Charles Tait	1906
RaceCam	Channel 7	1979
Winged keel	Ben Lexcen	1983
Fridge	James Harrison	1854
Electric drill	Arthur Arnot	1889
Splayd	William McArthur	1943
The Triton work centre	George Lewin	1976
Permanent crease clothing	CSIRO	1957
Communication and IT		
Polymer banknotes	The Reserve Bank, the CSIRO and the University of Melbourne	1988
Wi-Fi technology	CSIRO	1992
Google Maps	Lars and Jens Rasmussen	2004
Tools	Arthur Arnot	1889
Electric drill		
Military weapons		
Torpedo	Louis Brennan	1874

Even with this level of innovation, there are few industries that have developed. It's very difficult to name genuinely innovative global Australian businesses emerging. Cochlear (the bionic ear) and ResMed (CPAP) are two. There may be others. Many of our innovations and associated ideas have been licensed or the businesses sold to overseas interests instead. (Maybe we are an intellectual property hub.)

A classic case in point is our failure to commercialise Ian Frazer's cervical cancer vaccine. In his book, Frazer laments that if we'd been able to take that next step, the vaccine might have been on the market sooner. There would also have been estimated $300 million in increased annual revenue for Australia, as well as many more jobs created.[44] So the problem was...?

Wi-Fi is another. This ground-breaking Australian technology was commercialised by Sony and Microsoft.[45]

In the most recent surge of entrepreneurial activity, Australian start-ups Atlassian, Aconex and Canva stand out as 'unicorns'.[46,47] It is interesting to note that:

- Atlassian listed on NASDAQ,
- Aconex was sold to Oracle, and
- only Canva remains as an Australian business – for how long?

I suspect many Australians have never heard of these companies.

Contrast that situation with Sweden, a country of just 9.8 million people. Below is a list of Swedish brands that would be familiar to many Australians:

- Electrolux
- Volvo
- Ericsson

44 https://www.goodreads.com/book/show/18249781-ian-frazer, p. 167
45 https://www.abc.net.au/news/2010-08-14/concerns-raised-over-commercialised-csiro/943764
46 https://www.news.com.au/finance/business/technology/aussie-billiondollar-success-story/news-story/2d34de4afa8389ffda3fda6e19b5454d
47 https://www.afr.com/personal-finance/tech-unicorns-will-they-keep-soaring-or-are-valuations-fantasy-20180517-h10670

- IKEA
- Skype
- H&M
- Spotify

I wonder if any Australian brands would be household names in Sweden?

Just as interesting is the number of Australian businesses (and brands) which have been sold offshore in the past decade, including:

- Dulux (sold in 2019)
- Pacific Brands (2016)
- Toll (2015)
- Wendy's (2014)
- RM Williams (2013)
- Billabong (2012)
- Fosters (2011)
- Esky (2009)
- Golden Circle (2009).

The innovation and business development associated with now internationally owned companies like these occurred in Australia. Selling our businesses offshore might benefit a few shareholders in the short-term (and the professional services industry which benefits enormously), but it does nothing for the long-term prosperity of Australia as a whole.

Firms including lawyers, accountants, investment banks and venture capitalists make huge fees in commissions and services to put these deals together. But in whose best interest?

Maybe we are a business incubator for the world? This effectively means creating small businesses and selling them to the world. If that's what is decided, let's do it well. But much of our wealth is then exported.

For example, Australia has natural advantages in the area of food production, but we've been guilty of selling many major food production assets offshore, rather than capitalising on their long-term value and the prosperity they could deliver. There are many reasons for this, including globalisation and short-term shareholder greed, and maybe even a lack of competence or capacity.

At least 20 years ago when I was working in the food industry, I remember one industry leader 'screaming' in frustration that Asia (specifically Japan) was the major opportunity. He indicated that the market research in Japan was suggesting that food security was a major threat in their future and Australia should be the 'food bowl of Asia'. While we cannot supply all their needs, there is no doubt it is a huge market opportunity. We know for sure that at least some Australian food companies have since been bought by Japanese (and Chinese) interests.

Australia has suffered from not commercially exploiting its innovation opportunities. We are stuck in an 'exporting commodities/processing raw materials' mindset. Other economies have progressed while we have not taken opportunities as they have arisen. It might be called complacency or even lack of imagination or foresight. The idea of vision- driven policy might be a proposition to discuss.

The Australian of the Year Awards

Reviewing the history of the Australian of the Year awards helps to shine a light on how business achievement is valued in this country. This award has been presented on Australia Day each year since 1960 and is our most visible recognition of leading Australians. An analysis over time shows the following award-winners by industry category.

- Sport (13)
- Science/Health (12)
- The Arts (11)
- Public/Military Service (8)
- Community Service/The Environment (5)
- Indigenous Leadership (4)
- Business (4)
- The Clergy (2)
- Academia (2).

What a revelation. The top three categories (Sport, the 'Health' component of Science/Health, and The Arts) are all lifestyle related. Lifestyle wins by the length of the straight.

While I have no doubt all the recipients are outstanding Australians and worthy recipients, where are the business leaders? There's only 4. For the record, they were Alan Bond (1978), Dick Smith (1986), Simon McKeon (2011) and Ita Buttrose (2013).

It is easy to understand why Science/Health is near the top of the list. The Arts is a major cultural activity. And Sport – it's because 'we punch above our weight'.

Business barely gets a mention – the one sector of society which (loosely speaking) funds everything. Is it that there are no worthy Australian business leaders or that we are not able to recognise them?

The debate in this country needs to more accurately reflect the fact that business and wealth creation are the platform for prosperity in Australia.

There is no doubt Australia deserves world-class education and health systems, the NDIS, the NBN, and a robust defence system. But none of these will exist without a great business system in place.

Some great work was done in the 1980s and 1990s to position Australia for the 21st century. Many nation-building measures were dismantled so the economy could be more responsive and flexible in the context of the global economy. This work included:

- floating the $
- the reduction in tariffs
- deregulation of the finance sector and
- restructuring the labour market.

These were all decisions which created turbulence and it was this period of restructuring that laid the groundwork for a period of unprecedented growth in Australia. 28 years of economic growth and counting. The restructuring also provided the basis for Australia to manage the global financial crisis of 2008.

Is it possible to engage in that level of restructuring again?

Do we have any idea what we are restructuring to?

Who is leading this debate?

My view is that the work is starting as we speak. There are industry plans. There is a focus on start-ups, and the 'gig' economy is with us, but the work needs to be more visible. If we do not accelerate our rate of change (learning), there will come a time when the global economy will do it for us. We'll benefit as a whole if we work together to manage our own destiny.

But what is happening? Over the last decade we've had a succession of governments who are a captive of the here and now, and who appear to be unable to lead a genuine conversation about the future. It might even be suggested there has been no genuine economic reform since the late 1990s.

Maybe one day we'll wake up.

Key Points

- Australian innovations have changed the world (like Gardasil), but we have missed many opportunities to commercialise them.
- Economic restructuring in Australia in the 1980s laid the platform for 28 consecutive years of economic growth.
- Only four business leaders have won the Australian of the Year Award (which started in 1960).

PART TWO
Our Current Position

Chapter 2
AUSTRALIA'S BUSINESS CULTURE

"Australia must diversify its economy by investing in highly skilled workers and become the knowledge nation to stop us slipping out of the top 20 economies."

—Jeremy Thorpe[48]

Introduction

This chapter analyses the elements of Australia's business culture. Australia is now the 13th largest economy in the world and the services sector accounts for 75% of our value-adding and 88% of employment.[49] We are a long way from the 'farm' and 'quarry' metaphors of our past. Major changes in our industry base have changed the culture of Australian business.

The Australian business culture has many elements. Some of the more obvious elements include:

1. our industry and employment composition.
2. the scale of our businesses – small, medium, and large.
3. the range of different business structures – public companies, private companies and the different variations within them, such as family businesses, government- owned enterprises and statutory systems.
4. the industrial relations system – including awards, regulatory bodies and trade unions.
5. the range of industry associations that exist in Australia.

A review of each of these components in more detail provides an insight into our business culture.

---

48 https://www.theaustralian.com.au/business/latest/aust-on-a-slippery-slope-pwc/news-story/66b131953959980e61d26c231400cf02

49 https://www.austrade.gov.au/International/Invest/Resources/Benchmark-Report

Our Industry and Employment Composition

There is no question that our wealth in the past has come from the agricultural and resource sectors. But today the Australian economy is a diversified services economy. The table below shows the employment spread over our major industry sectors and the gross value-added contributions of each sector:[50]

Industry	Employed persons %	Gross Value-Added
Health Care and Social Assistance	13.3	7.9
Retail Trade	10.0	4.8
Construction	9.4	8.1
Professional, Scientific Technical Services	8.5	7.4
Education and Training	7.9	5.2
Manufacturing	7.7	6.3
Accommodation and Food Services	7.0	2.6
Public Administration and Safety	6.4	5.7
Transport Postal and Warehousing	5.1	5.1
Financial and Insurance Services	3.6	9.5
Admin and Support Services	3.1	3.4
Wholesale Trade	2.9	4.4
Agriculture Forestry Fishing	2.6	2.6
Mining	1.9	6.4
Info. Media and Telecommunications	1.8	2.9
Electricity, Gas, and Waste Services	1.2	2.6
Other Services	7.6	5.9

50 https://www.austrade.gov.au/International/Invest/Resources/Benchmark-Report

Approximately 43% of Australia's workforce now has a tertiary education and more than a third of Australian employees were born in another country.[51]

The transition to a services economy is over. It has been over for a long time. When 75% of our "Gross Value-Added" is based on the service economy and 80% of the employment in Australia is in the services economy, it's fair to say we are a services economy. Those who believe we are transitioning to a services economy are at least 10 years behind.

The fact that our manufacturing sector is small is also significant. Andrew Liveris (the Australian former Chairman and CEO of American multinational Dow Chemical Company) has suggested that most global innovation comes from the manufacturing sector.

"Innovation is most successful when it goes hand in hand with production, particularly in the advanced manufacturing sector. In fact, a recent McKinsey study found that manufacturing accounts for up to 90 per cent of private sector R&D in major manufacturing economies.

This is one of the reasons I have championed advanced manufacturing in every corner of the world for many years. Because the solutions we seek... the solutions that will drive sustainable growth and human progress... will be found at the intersection of innovation and production.

Australia, to be frank, is behind in this area. As you know, we have allowed our manufacturing sector to shrivel in recent years... settling for an economy defined by exporting natural resources.

Do not get me wrong – this approach has produced incredible growth in the short term. However, overemphasising extraction and export – at the expense of other priorities – has clear downsides."[52]

The link between innovation and the manufacturing sector (only 6.3% of the economy), is critical.

51 https://www.austrade.gov.au/International/Invest/Resources/Benchmark-Report
52 Extract from Andrew Liveris' speech at the AICD Leaders' Edge Luncheon, Brisbane, August 14, 2014.

The Scale of Businesses – Small, Medium and Large

While there is no doubt that corporate Australia plays a major role in the Australian economic landscape, a review of the scale of business reveals that we are a nation of small businesses:

- 97% of businesses employ less than 20 people (and 89% of those employ less than 4)
- 2.4% of businesses employ between 20 and 199 people
- 0.3% of businesses employ more than 200 people.

The small and medium-sized businesses of Australia are an incredibly important part of our wealth-creation process.

There are times when I have considered that the Australian business imagination is limited by the fact that we are a geographically remote island in Asia. Our geographic isolation combined with our incredible natural resources has allowed us to avoid some of the big issues of economic survival that other countries face. We have created a level of self-sufficiency which has allowed us to remain inward looking and egocentric in our perspectives about the future.

The Range of Business Structures

Public companies

The top 10 Australian Securities Exchange (ASX) publicly listed companies and their founding dates are listed in the table below.

1	BHP/Billiton (1885)
2	Commonwealth Bank (1911)
3	Westpac (1817)
4	ANZ (1835)
5	NAB (1893)
6	Telstra (1901)
7	CSL (1916)
8	Wesfarmers (1914)
9	Woolworths (1924)
10	Macquarie Bank (1970)

Here are some other important facts about this grouping of companies:

- four were founded before Federation
- five were founded by Government
- all were founded before 1970
- nine were founded prior to 1924
- five are banks
- value-adding businesses are limited (my count is one, maybe two).

Our list is at odds with the corresponding US Top 10 list, which features five companies founded since 1970. It's no surprise that all five are technology-based: Microsoft (1975), Apple (1976), Amazon (1994), Alphabet (Google, 1998), and Facebook (2004).[53] Here's another confronting fact: 52% of the top 500 public companies in the US have disappeared in the last 15 years.[54]

It might be argued that the Australian economy is 'old' and lacking in an entrepreneurial spirit.[55] It might also be suggested that it was (and is) government dependent, and at some level, government funded. The fact that Australia is gifted with abundant natural resources, while a great blessing, has caused a myopia which is limiting.

Private companies

The top 10 private companies in Australia and their founding dates are provided in the following table.[56]

53 https://www.cnbc.com/2017/03/08/the-top-10-us-companies-by-market-capitalization.html

54 https://us1.campaign-archive.com/?u=0c60818e26ecdbe423a10ad2f&id=478fd40ea8&e=3c4e719690

55 http://www.smh.com.au/small-business/entrepreneur/bernard-salt-warns-australia-lacks-entrepreneurial-spirit-20170901-gy8oa4.html

56 https://www.afr.com/leadership/afr-lists/top-500-private-companies/top-500-private-companies-2018-the-full-list-20180903-h14w4v

1	Visy (1948)
2	Hancock Prospecting (1955)
3	7-Eleven (first Australian store opened in 1977)
4	CBH Group (1933)
5	Meriton (1963)
6	BGC (1960)
7	Hutchies (1912)
8	HCF (1932)
9	Teys (1946)
10	Cotton On Group (1991)

And here are some other important facts about this grouping of companies:

- only two started post-1970
- two are/were membership-based organisations
- only two are genuinely value-adding businesses (Visy and Teys. Teys is 50% owned by the American-based Cargill company).

The 20 companies in the two tables above are symbols of our business culture. They are the leaders. As a whole, they are symbolic of an Australian business culture.

There are some further interesting facts about private companies in Australia:

- family businesses constitute around 70% of all businesses in Australia.
- many family businesses survive for generations, and the average length of time of operation of family businesses in Australia is 34 years.
- the average age of family business owners is 58 and 25% are aged over 65.
- 26% of family businesses are in the second generation of ownership and 14% are in a third generation or more.[57]

There is also some specific research highlighting that not all people in the small business sector are entrepreneurs. In a survey conducted by the

57 https://www.familybusinesshub.com.au/what-is-family-business

Cameron Research group the following groupings emerged:[58]

- passionate professionals – 32%
- business builders – 20%
- lifestyle seekers – 48%.

No surprise there – 48% are lifestyle seekers. As the SME sector is a major contributor to our economy this reflects our business culture.

The Industrial Relations System

Business culture in Australia cannot be discussed without considering the impact of the trade unions and our industrial relations system. The trade union movement evolved well before Federation with unions being formed in the early-to-mid 1800s. As it evolved, the movement developed two arms: the trade union arm and the political arm – the Australian Labor Party.

Australia's industrial system evolved to include an award system to protect the rights of workers and a court system which arbitrates disputes. Some achievements of the union system include:

- the right of workers to form a union which elects its own independent representatives
- the introduction of awards to ensure that employers observe minimum wages and working conditions
- equal pay
- long service leave
- pay loading for evenings, nights and weekends
- paid public holidays
- periodic wage increases
- maternity/adoption/parental leave
- annual leave and leave loading
- protective clothing and equipment provided by employers

58 https://mailchi.mp/f7304e40795b/the-growth-myth

- workplace health and safety laws
- compensation for work-related injury
- occupational superannuation
- the right of employees to be given notice and to be consulted about changes at work (for example, the introduction of new technology, planned retrenchments, and new working arrangements)
- personal carer's leave.[59]

There have also been significant trade union disputes in Australia's relatively recent industrial relations history, including the SEQEB dispute in Queensland in the mid-1980s and the pilots' strike in 1989. In the late 1990s, there was also the waterfront dispute. These disputes all contributed to the deregulation and increasing flexibility of the Australian workplace.

The influence of trade unions on Australia has been (and is) important. However, union membership has declined significantly in Australia over recent decades. There are many reasons for this, including:

- the abolition of compulsory unionism
- changing industry structures
- a better educated workforce
- younger workers perceiving less trade union relevance
- Australia having enjoyed 28 years of interrupted economic growth (i.e. good times).

Declining union membership is a more complex issue than can be addressed here. However, it is vital that unions find a focus that extends beyond the traditional redistribution of wealth to one that has a more wholistic view which includes wealth creation and prosperity. In my view there is a role for unions to play in the business system, but it will require a radical rethink of their mission. The world of work has changed – why are unions not leading at least some of the thinking about the change? The 'gig' economy is an example.

59 https://www.actu.org.au/about-the-actu/history

The Range of Industry Associations in Australia

There are a range of business associations representing large business in Australia, such as the Business Council of Australia and the Australian Industry Group. Others represent SMEs, such as the Council of Small Business Organisations Australia, as well as various professions (e.g. the Australian Institute of Company Directors and various professional bodies for accountants and medical practitioners).

All of these groupings have a position of influence and an agenda in the business debates. They are influencers in determining, contributing to (and even defining) the business culture in Australia. Some might even claim a leadership role in the Australian policy debate around issues like labour market deregulation, taxation, employee benefits and technology.

If we look back to the initial politics of Australia, the great political divide at Federation was free trade versus protection. The political parties of the day actually lined up around these issues. These same issues remain today. However, our political parties today do not have the same policy clarity. In recent years the debates about the car industry, the defence industries (e.g. submarines) and free trade agreements all have echoes of the founding debates of Australia.

The challenge for Australian business now is to lead Australia into a new era of prosperity – there are early signs of this emerging as I write. New generations of entrepreneurs and entrepreneurial ecosystems are forming with start-up hubs, accelerators, landing pads and the emergence of unicorns (start-ups that are valued at over $1 billion). There is a whole new language appearing. In my lifetime I have not seen this level of activity. The question is: can these early shoots survive the 'Australian business culture'?

Key Points

- Australia is a service-based economy.
- Not one of our top 10 publicly-listed companies was founded after 1970.
- 70% of all Australian businesses are family businesses.
- Research indicates that only 20% of small businesses are 'business builders'.

Chapter 3

AUSTRALIA'S CURRENT PERFORMANCE (and what we can learn from it)

"Confront the brutal Facts (yet never lose faith)."

—James Collins[60]

Introduction

This chapter analyses Australia's current economic and business performance on a range of international indices. I also offer perspectives on what we can learn from our comparative performance. But first, let me talk about another index.

Australia came tenth (out of 206) in the medal tally at the 2016 Rio Olympics.[61] But there was a general feeling lead by the media that our athletes had failed in Rio. There were predictable calls for funding to be increased to maintain 'Australia's sporting reputation'.[62] John Wylie (the chair of Sport Australia) and Matt Carroll (the chief executive of the Australian Olympic Committee) have said that without increased federal government funding, the nation's global sporting reputation will be lost.[63] (Is 10th a poor result?)

Contrast those sentiments with the reaction to the 'innovation agenda' that former Prime Minister Malcolm Turnbull enthusiastically announced soon after taking office in 2015. Turnbull had been a successful businessman and understood the value of innovation. But fast-forward to 2016 and the then Industry, Innovation and Science Minister (Arthur Sinodinos) stated that *"the government took an election shellacking because its objective to drive a more entrepreneurial society did not resonate with everyday Australians"*.[64]

60 https://www.goodreads.com/author/show/2826.James_C_Collins
61 http://www.espn.com.au/olympics/summer/2016/medals
62 https://www.abc.net.au/news/2019-01-04/more-funding-needed-to-maintain-australian-sporting-reputation/10686406
63 https://www.abc.net.au/news/2019-01-04/more-funding-needed-to-maintain-australian-sporting-reputation/10686406
64 https://www.afr.com/news/policy/turnbull-innovation-agenda-was-a-political-failure-government-concedes-20170919-gyk617

Australians are preconditioned to consider recreation as a priority. Not only that, we seem to derive the core of our national identity from sport. For example:

- 'the whole country' stops in November for the Melbourne Cup.
- Phar Lap is iconic.
- Don Bradman is legendary.
- Each capital city has a number of statues of sporting identities to celebrate their iconic status.

Do other countries have this preoccupation with sport?

In a society where sport is paramount, what happens to business and wealth creation – the sector which enables our lifestyle? It was suggested that the government of the day got a 'shellacking' because the innovation debate did not resonate. Maybe there were other factors? Our future lifestyle depends on a robust growing business sector with entrepreneurship and innovation as key elements.

The Pursuit of Mediocrity

In terms of business rankings, a range of global indices are published each year that provide comparative rankings about the business environment in different countries.

The following table, highlights how Australia stacks up on a range of global indices:

The Index	What it measures	Our Ranking
Good Country Index[65]	What each country on earth contributes to the common good of humanity	20th
Legatum Prosperity Index[66]	A range of factors including wealth, economic growth, education levels, personal health, wellbeing and quality of life	17th
Social Progress Index[67]	A range of factors including health care, infrastructure and civil liberties	15th
Global Competitiveness Index[68]	How internationally competitive our industries are	16th

65 https://www.goodcountry.org/index/results
66 https://www.prosperity.com/
67 https://www.socialprogress.org/index/global/results
68 https://www.weforum.org/reports/how-to-end-a-decade-of-lost-productivity-growth

The Index	What it measures	Our Ranking
Global Innovation Index[69]	How innovative we are	23rd
Global Entrepreneurship Index[70]	How entrepreneurial we are (an early sign of things to come?)	5th
Ease of Doing Business Index[71]	How easy it is do business in Australia	14th
Manufacturing Index[72]	The value added to our GDP by manufacturing	103rd
Manufacturing Self-Sufficiency[73]	How self-sufficient we are in terms of what we manufacture	Last
Economic Complexity[74]	The productive capabilities of our economy	93rd

Australia's Economic Complexity Index is now 93 which is a ranking decrease of 7 in the last 12 months. Over a generation our ranking has dropped substantially. This Index is an indicator of economic growth and prosperity in the future. It highlights *"a measure of knowledge in a society that gets translated into the products it makes. A country is considered 'complex' if it exports not only highly complex products (determined by the Product Complexity index) but also a large number of different products. The more complex a country's index, the stronger its infrastructure and the more adaptable it is to market changes."*[75]

The ranking indicates our economy is getting simpler each year. It means there is less value added by Australian business. Why is that?

Indices like this should have the whole Australian business system asking questions of our future industries and their capacity to create wealth. A ranking of 93 moving downwards is alarming.

It is way less than the 10th position we achieved in the Olympics. Can you imagine if our ranking after the Olympics was 93? A national outrage?

69 https://www.wipo.int/global_innovation_index/en/2020/
70 https://thegedi.org/global-entrepreneurship-and-development-index/
71 https://www.doingbusiness.org/en/rankings
72 https://www.theglobaleconomy.com/rankings/Share_of_manufacturing/
73 https://www.abc.net.au/news/2020-07-23/coronavirus-pandemic-leads-to-australian-manufacturing-revival/12481568
74 https://www.abc.net.au/news/2019-11-02/australia-rich-and-dumb-or-an-innovation-nation/11657984
75 http://atlas.cid.harvard.edu/

In comparative terms we rank with Senegal and Pakistan. Is that where we see ourselves in the future? In addition, the Australian Innovation System Report (2017) highlighted that *"Across a range of metrics on collaboration for innovation, Australia ranks in the bottom half of the OECD"*.

The Report also stated that *"Research and development (R&D) by Australia's businesses as a share of GDP has declined sharply since 2008–09, after strong growth in the previous decade."*[76]

A recent Senate sub-committee also found that only 30 per cent of Australia's research and development workforce is employed in industry, whereas this figure is closer to 80 per cent in advanced economies such as the US. Australia rates poorly internationally in terms of industry-led innovation.[77]

Surely these statistics are a wake-up call.

If Australia's performance at the Olympics is important, how is it that our business performance against other countries is not equally as important? For a country that expects a lot of its athletes, we seem to have very low performance expectations when it comes to the creation of prosperity and/or wealth creation through business.

In many of these areas Australia's performance has declined over recent years. Are we upset? Not really. The items pass through the news cycle almost without comment. The Olympics however is a different story. Somehow, we believe we are a sporting nation and we set the bar high in every sport. The Olympics is our test and a debate about strategy and funding is a form of therapy for the country. So why doesn't a debate like that happen for innovation and commercialisation in Australia?

Sadly, there appears to be little public understanding or acceptance that Australia's survival and prosperity into the middle of the 21st century will only come off the back of a successful business sector. It is business that does the heavy lifting to create jobs and prosperity. Governments can only create the conditions for it to occur. But the role of government is critical.

76 Australian Innovation System Report 2017.
77 https://www.aph.gov.au/Parliamentary_Business/Committees/Senate/Economics/Innovation_System/Report/c02

In her work *The Entrepreneurial State,* Mariana Mazzucato highlights a number of instances (from the iPhone to clean energy) where the government has taken a lead with bold risky investments and in time private business investment followed. The story about the iPhone is a classic. She highlights Steve Jobs' Stanford University address where he talks about *"pursuing what you love"* and *"staying foolish"*.

According to Mazzucato, this story about Apple *"creates the myth about the origin of Apple's success. Individual genius, attention to design, a love for play, and foolishness were no doubt important characteristics. But without the massive amount of public investment behind the computer and internet revolutions, such attributes might have led only to a new toy, not the cutting-edge revolution products like the iPad and the iPhone which have changed the way people work and communicate."*[78]

In Australia, our governments have a mixed record at supporting pioneering technology. Many opportunities have been missed through lack of foresight, lack of political courage, complacency or incompetence. It might be argued that government sees R&D and higher education as a cost rather than an investment.

Without an outstanding successful business sector there are no products and services of any substance, no jobs, no taxes and very little wealth – ultimately a very poor society. The absence of substantial corporate headquarters is another limiting factor on our innovative capacity.

One might ask – what about a visionary government?

In the 2019 election build-up, the two major parties produced one-page policy summaries. The Labor Party barely mentioned the one sector of the Australian community (business) which actually creates the wealth. Labor highlighted fairness as their theme. The Liberal Party at least had a focus on small business as the major wealth creation sector, along with a focus on regional Australia.

If our political parties have no coherent story on wealth creation and prosperity in the presentation of their policies, Australia does not have a story. The embarrassing revolving door of Prime Ministers that we have

78 https://marianamazzucato.com/entrepreneurial-state/, p. 87,88.

experienced over the past decade certainly hasn't helped fill the leadership vacuum. Our recent narrative has been more about 'musical chairs' or 'pass the parcel'. Our political system has been reduced to monthly popularity contests. How much time is wasted analysing these meaningless contests?

I sometimes wonder when politicians claim credit for job creation, if they actually have any understanding of what they are saying.

- Are they increasing the number of public servants being employed?
- Are they announcing a major publicly funded program (infrastructure or another project)?
- Or has business actually created jobs with some government support?

A modicum of intellectual integrity would have politicians acknowledge their real role. Business is the wealth-creation unit that creates the majority of jobs, especially the SME sector (businesses<199 people). What's even more important to understand is that the SME sector is the engine room of wealth creation and prosperity. I remember a time in Australia when unemployment was over 10% and there was discussion about a 'simple solution'. Each small business to employ one person – problem solved – millions of jobs. Oh, for such simplicity.

Government at a strategic level has the capacity to be a *"market creator or shaper"* according to Mazzucato.[79] In addition, she states that *"most of the radical, revolutionary innovations that have fueled the dynamics of capitalism – from railroads to the Internet, to modern day nanotechnology and pharmaceuticals – trace the most courageous early and capital-intensive entrepreneurial investments back to the State."*[80]

Government can and does play a major role in enhancing the business environment by investing in long-term R&D, building infrastructure and creating a favourable regulatory and tax environment.

In the event you doubt the power of business to create wealth, here's a powerful story to help convince you. Massachusetts Institute of Technology (MIT) is one of the world's most prestigious higher education

79 https://marianamazzucato.com/entrepreneurial-state/, p. 10
80 https://marianamazzucato.com/entrepreneurial-state/, p. 3

institutions. Did you know that the annual gross revenue of start-up companies founded by MIT graduates is larger than the annual GDP of all but nine countries in the world? If these companies were an economy, it would be the tenth largest in the world, positioned in between Russia and India.[81]

MIT alumni[82] have launched 30,200 active companies, employing roughly 4.6 million people, and generating roughly $1.9 trillion in annual revenues. This is an amazing achievement, but what is even more amazing is the measurement of the result.

Can you imagine a university (or even a government) actually measuring its performance based on the gross revenue of the 'built-for profit' companies that its living graduates have started? It is a radical measure. Interesting measures of an election term would be the number of 'for profit' businesses created from government funded R&D investment, and the number of jobs created in those businesses.

I attended the MIT Entrepreneur Development Program in 2010. It was a great experience. There were many highlights apart from the formal learning. There were teams of entrepreneurs from many countries all struggling with similar issues on their journey. Three incidents impressed me.

1. We toured MIT's on-campus business incubator which housed about 100 start-ups. It was certainly abuzz with energy and activity. They highlighted that Android Inc. was based there in its start-up phase prior to being acquired by Google.
2. In one lecture I sat next to a young MIT student who had joined our cohort as a guest. I discovered that she was doing a PhD in Mechanical Engineering. She had already registered a number of patents. She was working on her first start-up in MIT's business incubator (and she was only 28).
3. In a number of conversations, I had with MIT staff and students, the 'competitive' message conveyed both directly and indirectly was that MIT students started businesses, while Harvard University (which is in the same

81 http://executive.mit.edu/blog/mit-entrepreneurs-the-worlds-10th-largest-economy#.WA_7SKOr3Hc

82 http://executive.mit.edu/blog/mit-entrepreneurs-the-worlds-10th-largest-economy#.WA_7SKOr3Hc

geographic area) produced graduates who went and worked for existing corporations and financial institutions. The narrative was clear.

MIT has created its own entrepreneurial ecosystem, which is a core platform for their capacity to commercialise their research. In Australia, our record of commercialising our research is poor. As pointed out earlier in the chapter, 70% of our research scientists are employed in our universities.

There is a generation of research people in Australia who believe that the government should fund them for life. They compete for grants from a range of different government sources. But where do they create value? Publishing papers is one potentially valuable output of a research system and we are world leaders at that. (In 19 out of 22 scientific research fields, Australian scientific research publications averaged a relative impact of at least 20% above the global average.)[83]

However, a more commercial focus might ask the question that I raised earlier:

How many Australians are employed in 'for profit' businesses as a result of this research as opposed to being employed in the research itself?

If the researchers are as well-educated and as creative as they claim, they might be creating their own jobs – putting proposals to industry and working in industry to extend the boundaries of thinking. It is difficult to find businesses in Australia who actually fund research at scale. Why is that? Surely a country in the southern hemisphere, situated in Asia, with our characteristics, could be a business hub for major global corporations. Instead, many have moved R&D centres to Israel.

Commercialisation is now much more prominent with universities having commercialisation structures, For example, UniQuest at UQ. In 2018, Uniquest celebrated 100 start-ups created with UQ research since 1988.[84] The nature of this work is long term and high risk. Building a business from scratch is a major undertaking. The timeframes are decades, not days or weeks. We are building a platform for the future. (Or will the Australian culture subsume these start-ups?) Do we know how many need to be founded for one to survive?

83 Australia Benchmark Report 2019, p. 35.
84 https://www.uniquest.com.au/news/celebrating-100-uq-startups-grow-jobs-and-queenslands-future

A colleague of mine who has founded a number of businesses was fond of using the analogy of baby sea turtles where the punch line is that only 1 in 1000 hatchlings will survive to adulthood.

Where is Australia's Business Future?

What are the current visions for Australia's business future? They are very difficult to articulate:

- a position in Asia?
- a defence industry (submarines)?
- an emerging story around Northern Australia?
- the healthiest nation in the world?

As we saw with Malcolm Turnbull's innovation agenda, these visions are so vague that they are unlikely to inspire a nation. Australia/Australian business needs to develop a great narrative about the future – some 'moon shots' that galvanise ordinary Australians.

My definition of a 'moon shot' is as follows: *A transformative nation-building statement of intent with a 30-50-year timeframe that has bipartisan support and focuses on:*

- *developing our contribution to humanity, and/or*
- *building major physical infrastructure that creates (or provides a vehicle for the creation of) national prosperity.*

'Moon shots' can provide us with a context for some of the big conversations we must have and the questions we must answer. Questions like:

- what are the industries that will drive our future?
- which industries will create the platform for many thousands of hi-tech, high-skilled jobs that will cultivate work and long-term careers for the next generations?
- how might we create a culture where business innovation and commercialisation is acknowledged as the equivalent of a 'national sport'?

I believe that we don't even have the language or the culture to discuss it.

When we talk about the big business issues in Australia, we talk about:

- tax reform – and then do nothing or play at the edges
- debts and deficits – every government has them, the debate is how big?
- growth and jobs – these issues are really a joint business/government agenda
- immigration – again the debate is about how many or about whether Australia is able to sustain more people
- education – of course it is a good thing and we need more of it
- productivity – we are among the leaders in the world
- innovation and agility – we are not among the leaders in the world.

Most of these topics are generalised and focus on some of the means to Australia becoming a prosperous country. But it seems no one is willing to lead a conversation about what Australia looks like as a great country post-2050. Our business leaders are virtually absent in conversations about the future in the current political and economic debate. That's not surprising given the general lack of trust in the business sector overall.

As one commentator recently said:

"But to restore public trust our business sector must also clean up its act. There are too many second-rate business executives doing a third-rate job. They should 'stick to their knitting' instead of running to the government for help or blaming the trade unions.

In the end it is not companies that perform well or badly. It is people. They must be held accountable, particularly directors and senior executives."[85]

It is a bruising comment.

The CSIRO has been a catalyst for attempting to discuss Australia's future over the past decade. It has published four potential scenarios in their

85 http://johnmenadue.com/john-menadue-the-failings-of-our-corporate-sector-and-not-just-the-banks-and-insurance-companies/

Australia 2030: Navigating Our Uncertain Future report. But that report came and went in the media cycle in a blip. For the record, their four scenarios are listed below.

1. **Digital DNA**

   "Australia experiences a dramatic shift towards a digital services and knowledge-driven economy made possible by the exponential growth of computing power, an increasingly connected world, and the wide range of new technologies this enables."

2. **Mining and Dining**

   "Australia's economy benefits from a second wave of the resources boom driven by growth and urbanisation in developing economies. Minerals, energy and food represent the majority of Australian exports and are the underpinning wealth generators for the economy."

3. **Clean and Lean**

   "Decoupling of economic growth and environmental sustainability has led countries to simultaneously pursue both objectives. Consumers seek out healthier lifestyles and Australia works with other advanced economies to address carbon abatement, resource efficiency and sustainability."

4. **Weathering the Storm**

   "Global geopolitical instability increases, driven by climate change and regional conflicts over access to land, food and water. Tensions threaten to destabilise trade alliances and disrupt global supply chains, leading to prolonged global economic stagnation."

Scenario planning is a tool to enable businesses and communities to consider the future in a creative and disciplined way. Given the future by definition is unknowable, scenario planning enables groups to consider multiple futures and so to prepare for multiple possibilities and opportunities. I can only hope this CSIRO work is front and centre in the planning for many Australian businesses.

There are many challenges and we know that technology is changing the world. For example:

- mines in Western Australia are being managed remotely and an autonomous train that is officially the world's largest robot is making iron ore deliveries from the mines.[86]

- Uber and Airbnb have disrupted our transport and accommodation industries.
- driverless vehicles are in the foreseeable future.
- we are on the edge of the world becoming a cashless society.
- whole new industries are emerging. For example, who had heard of 'FinTech' or 'EdTech' five years ago? Or 'Esports'?

Technology is evolving at a rapid pace. However, little direction/vision (or what is now popularly described as a 'narrative') is being provided on how Australia can navigate these challenges. If a vision for Australia is too broad, we could at least have a series of industry visions?

Unfortunately, providing these visions is challenging in a culture where our capacity to see beyond our 'problems' is limited. We have become a nation of hypercritical cynics. We actually revel in the process of defining ourselves by our problems, whatever they happen to be. It has been that way for a long time and as they say – misery loves company.

Anyone who dares to articulate a big dream is laughed at, demeaned, and generally maligned – then if they happen to be politicians they are belittled and they get caught in a never-ending game of broken promises and 'gotcha' moments by journalists, who have done little in their lives but be armchair critics.

Who would want to lead in this country? As a country our culture is so insular, cautious and tradition-bound that we are actually fearful of the future so we 'cut down' our leaders and export our great ideas offshore. It might be argued our imagination is limited by cultural constraints and the fact that we are an island.

There was a time when Australia engaged in 'nation-building' projects: The Snowy Mountains Scheme, the national road and rail systems, the ports and the creation of corporations such as the Post Office, the Australian Broadcasting Corporation, the Commonwealth Bank, the CSIRO, Telstra, QANTAS – and more recently CSL and Cochlear. These projects emerged out of visionary government policies.

86 https://www.businessinsider.com.au/rio-tinto-robot-iron-iron-ore-2018-7

As a nation, our capabilities are limited only by our imagination and by 'political will'. Can anyone name any current visionary policy? Perhaps the recent decision to re-enter the space industry is one.[87] (And the decision to join the world as one of the top 10 arms manufacturers is another.)[88] It appears though that recent governments have lacked the will to engage in ambitious behaviour.

Yet it is hard to name any 'nation-building' projects of substance emerging in the last 20 years – perhaps only the NBN. It should have had bipartisan support as a long-term nation-building project. It appears that the Labor Party had little idea about the nature and scale of the project when they conceived it, and the Liberal Party subsequently wanted to deconstruct it in a way that positioned them politically. We now have a 'second grade' broadband system and our internet speeds are 60th in the world.[89] Given that this type of technology is changing the world, surely a country as sophisticated as Australia should be among the world leaders.

In a country where we are well educated and have an advanced democratic system in place, I wonder why we struggle with:

1. **making decisions about building major infrastructure**

   For example, the Very Fast Train conversation continues. It's been going on for decades. And the Western Sydney Airport decision was only made after a 30-plus-year conversation.

2. **long-term water issues**

   At primary school we were taught that Australia is the driest continent – but there have been few significant water projects initiated since the Snowy Mountains Scheme (other than Snowy 2.0 and the Ord River Irrigation Scheme.) The desalination plants which were built in a panic during our last water crises appear to now be 'white elephants'. How many billions were spent?

87 https://australianaviation.com.au/2019/03/adelaide-getting-two-new-space-facilities/

88 https://www.scmp.com/news/asia/australasia/article/2131008/australias-bold-plan-become-one-worlds-top-10-arms-exporters

89 https://finance.nine.com.au/2018/01/08/10/17/australias-fixed-internet-speed-ranking-falls-two-places-to-55th

3. **wealth creation (increasing the size of the pie)**

   As a country we are wonderfully good at discussing and debating how our national wealth should be redistributed. However, we are incapable of an intelligent conversation about the creation of wealth.

4. **the 'globalisation' of population**

   In a world of 7 billion heading to 9 billion people, Australia surely cannot believe we can continue with the same divisive debates which are currently the standard. Whether it is about refugees, immigration or 'Big Australia', we seem unable to have a thoughtful conversation.

5. **building 'infrastructure' in a public/private partnership**

   The media go into meltdown when these ventures don't make a profit quickly.

6. **having a genuine political debate about anything of substance.**

   The political system is devoted to spin and talking points and means, not ends. The media is devoted to instant entertainment and 'gotcha' moments. Issues are then let die because of a 24-hour news cycle.

It may be argued that our leaders lack the ability to articulate a vision for Australia. It might be argued that leaders in Australia are unwilling to articulate a genuine vision for Australian business because the business and political risks are too high. From my perspective, a big part of the problem is that as a country we are too comfortable: 'we are committed to lifestyle'.

The baby-boomer generation (whose time has passed), has wanted for little and at some level are happy to cruise along with a well-developed sense of cynicism and an overdeveloped sense of criticism. The Gen Xs and Gen Ys are leading in a very different environment.

The prevalence of the various social media platforms combined with the emergence of new technology is changing the world in ways which are both unimaginable and profound. These developments, along with the emergence of Asia (China) and India, massive population shifts, and the decline of major cultural pillars is creating a turbulence which is unsettling. This environment is a whole new challenge. The US Army describes it as volatile, uncertain, complex and ambiguous (VUCA).

Our current approach appears to be to continue doing what we are doing – have never- ending debates about the means of doing things and not have real conversations about Australia as a prosperous nation in the second half of the 21st century. We deny, avoid or close down major issues (i.e. those which 'create controversy or discomfort'), while other politically acceptable but less important issues often command lots of attention. We are creating groupings of 'ideological cripples' and 'intellectual pygmies' who seem to thrive on a game based on hand-grenade throwing.

How can we have a national conversation about what sort of a country we want in 50-60-70 years' time? More creativity in required in our use of social technology. There was a time when Australia was a 'social laboratory' – a world leader. Why not now?

A proposal – convene a Prosperity Commission. (We have much expertise at Royal Commissions). The purpose: to consider a range of questions on Prosperity for Australia in 2075.

What will Australia look like as a prosperous country in 2075?

The decisions we make in the next decade will influence that, but unfortunately the concept of coming together to agree on major national issues seems to be a 'bridge too far'.

However, we do have the Australian Sports Commission with a permanent brief to ensure Australia remains competitive in the global sporting arena over time.

Sport as a Metaphor – What Business Can Learn from Sport

This chapter began by highlighting the levels of performance that Australians tend to demand from our professional athletes. Australian business could learn a lot from Australian sport and how it's evolved in the professional era. For example:

- player performance is now measured at micro levels; metres run, kicks completed, missed tackles, hit-ups, hand balls, passes, and the list goes on. Those stats are in addition to the old macro measures of scrums won, tries or runs scored, wickets taken, and goals kicked.

- there are coaching teams with each coach focusing on different facets of a game – there's not only a head coach, there's a fitness coach, a kicking coach, an attacking coach, a defensive coach, psychologists – you name it, anything to gain a high-performance edge.

Businesses like to use sport as a metaphor when it suits them, but when it comes to actually following similar high-performance principles, the follow-up is often weak or non-existent.

In fact, in most businesses there is little conversation about high performance and even less about the creation of prosperity and the contribution a business can make to the community. The dialogue in so many businesses is focused around profitability, shareholder value or solving the next problem.

The real purpose of business – serving a need in the market by serving a customer – is lost in the mire. Who holds the focus on the real purpose of business? In theory the leaders. It is here the sporting metaphor is useful. It is no secret that many business leaders have coaches – Steve Jobs had one. There is a suggestion that no-one has ever achieved high performance without a coach.

My management consulting practice actually morphed into a coaching practice over a number of years. I just responded to the demand of many clients who wanted me to engage with them and their staff over an extended period of time. It started in the early 1980s in a time when business coaching was non-existent in Australia.

However, now coaches are a phenomenon in business and there is limited staff training. The actual pursuit of high performance is often ignored or given lip service. Why? Maybe there is little understanding of what high performance in business actually is, other than in financial terms and even then, the understanding is limited.

It appears to me that most businesses pursue mediocrity with great passion. Some just survive from year to year. Below are some common differences between professional sport and business.

Sport	Business
Sporting teams and elite Individuals have always had coaches.	Only in recent years coaching has emerged as 'fashionable' (and then only for select senior people).
90 per cent of their time and resources is spent on training.	A very low percentage of their money and time is spent on training.
Grand finals every year are a big event. And there are 'higher levels' (e.g. representative teams).	At the end of the financial year, there is often no serious ritual to celebrate performance (high or otherwise) Annual General Meetings (AGMs) are close, although not always a celebration.
There is clear measurement of performance on a number of levels.	There is often only one measure –profitability. And no real benchmarking.
A major focus is on improving performance via set moves, discipline and repetitive training drills.	There is some focus on improving performance, but it's often limited to one-on-one discussions and maybe some training.
Great games, great teams, and great performances are acknowledged – even ritualised. There are statues of great players and horses.	Greatness is almost never talked about. In some cases, there are rewards for long service, and Christmas celebrations.
Overall rankings are clear and pathways to the elite level are very well mapped out.	There is often nothing specific – maybe a limited 'career path' for selected individuals.
Awards and rewards are clear and transparent (grand finals, Brownlow medals etc.).	There is usually limited acknowledgement – perhaps some national awards or some awards within businesses.

If business was serious about high performance, surely, they would apply the same (or similar) disciplines as professional sporting teams?

High performance in sport (and in business) requires many things. Strategic recruitment and development are just two. For example, in sport, children with talent or potential are discovered and encouraged (selected) to join elite programs. They may join an academy and spend a great deal of time focusing on their sport in conjunction with their schoolwork.

From there, they may go to a full-time program and play in a 'satellite' league until the time comes and they are selected to join a very elite group who make it to the big time. The whole focus of these programs is to develop elite athletes who can perform at high levels over a long period of time.

But where does this long-term development happen in business? Certainly, in my time at school, business was not even mentioned as a career option. I know it is very different now. For example, there are pathways like those provided by Young Achievement Australia.[90] Entrepreneurship is now also a major theme in the curriculum in some high schools.

These might be contributing factors in the recent emergence of the start-up culture in Australia. Business certainly has more focus in education now than at any time in the past.

In major corporates, there is no doubt some development for 'high potential staff', but for most businesses, at best there is an effort to get the best candidate from those who apply in the recruitment phase. After that, most are left to their own devices unless there is a specific development program in place (which there often isn't). Instead, management are focused on getting the work done and making money. While the idea of management and leaders as coaches is emerging, in most business environments it is a myth.

The bottom line is that we need a business sector which is out-performing the rest of the world so we can continue our lifestyle-driven culture. When I think about Australian business culture, it's tough to identify the 'iconic' leaders in Australian business – those who not only lead or have led their businesses, but those who provide leadership to the country.

Whether you agree with him or not, 1986 Australian of the Year Dick Smith is a passionate Australian and he has a position about our future. Phillip Ruthven and Bernard Salt are social commentators who also make a positive contribution to thinking about our future – on business specifically and Australia more broadly. The Myer family are making a serious contribution to the leadership conversation in Australia through the Cranlana Program.

There are few other business leaders actually leading a national conversation about the future.

---

90 http://www.jaaustralia.org

Creating Learning Organisations

In the early 1990s, Peter Senge wrote *The Fifth Discipline.* This book articulated the concept of the learning organisation and it was an idea of the moment.[91] The concept of an organisation that detected and corrected its own errors was first talked about in the 1970s. As these silver bullets tend to come and go – it went.

However, the concept that a business' capacity to learn may be the only competitive advantage it has is still relevant, and not just to businesses, possibly to communities and nations as well. I wonder what a 'learning nation' looks like in the 21st Century.

The rate of change now is exponentially greater. Thomas Friedman articulated a very strong case for lifelong learning in his most recent book *Thank You for Being Late.*[92]

Lifelong learning is not a new concept, but in the next century accelerated learning is a challenging new perspective. Work as we know (or knew) it is being transformed – learning is the new work. New work paradigms are evolving. We have already seen a guaranteed minimum income piloted in at least one European economy. There will be other models. It is no accident that Google and Apple are building campuses. Work and learning are now synonymous.

We need new language systems to frame our discussions about work. Some examples are provided in the table on the next page.

Changing mental maps

Traditional view	Emerging view
work as a source of money	work as a source of learning
work as isolated from the rest of life	work as integrated with life
work as meaningless	work as meaningful
work as drudgery and boredom	work as an opportunity to co-create with others
work as reactive and making others rich	work as a contribution to society making everyone prosperous

91 https://www.goodreads.com/book/show/255127.The_Fifth_Discipline
92 https://www.goodreads.com/book/show/26114127-thank-you-for-being-late

The concept of learning as a structured training event off-site is another model which needs to be challenged. I wrote about learning models in a paper entitled *Creating a Learning Organisation*. The key differences between traditional training and effective organisational learning are summarised in the table below.

Traditional training	Organisational (business) learning
conducted off-site with individuals or workgroups	occurs in the work environment with the work group
hierarchical	collegial
trainer has little contact with the work group manager	learning environment created with the workgroup in a learning/task process – there may be a learning facilitator (or a coach) involved
centred around a trainer or teacher	centered on the work or the workgroup in a self-directed process
content and skill-driven with an individual focus	work-driven group skill development is an output
very like traditional school systems	based on work-related problems and possibilities in the situation
skills are seen as separate from work	learning and skill development are seen as integral to work
may build individual commitment	builds organisational learning environment commitment
trainers' skill focus is on instruction (or at least, individual skill development)	trainers' focus is on enhancing managerial and workforce skills – both a task and a process focus
major focus on delivery of information, some focus on skill acquisition – minimal focus on process	balanced focus on results, the development of commitment and building a learning community/team
organisations viewed as mechanical structures	organisations viewed as fluid organic learning systems

The organisational learning model is being embraced by companies like Google and Apple who are building campuses at their head offices – those students who are moved to work in industry will have learning contracts and over a lifetime they will acquire 'learning accreditations', be they Applied Degrees, Diplomas or whatever the unit of educational accreditation is. The whole nature of universities is changing as we speak with external programs like Massive Open Online Courses (MOOCs) and the extraordinary resources available on YouTube and other media channels. Online programs and accreditations are accelerating.

The future for learning is only limited by the imagination of future generations.

Key Points

- Australia ranks outside the Top 10 on many global indices. We rank 93rd on the Economic Complexity Index.
- MIT alumni have launched 30,200 active companies, employing roughly 4.6 million people, and generating roughly $1.9 trillion in annual revenues.
- Business can learn from professional sport.
- Learning methods in the future will be very different.

Chapter 4
AUSTRALIA'S INNOVATION CONVERSATION

"As a nation, we're good at creating knowledge but simply not good enough at transferring or applying it."

—Bill Ferris[93]

Introduction

This chapter explains different ways of thinking about innovation and analyses a range of industry debates that have occurred in Australia in recent years. It also evaluates a plethora of reports that have been produced on innovation in Australia recent years.

A global innovation subculture has emerged using terms like start-ups, unicorns, accelerators, incubators and landing pads. There is a never-ending array of concepts to support the innovation conversation. If you don't know the language, you're not in it.

Australia actually ranked 5th in the 2018 Global Entrepreneurship Development Institute rankings, which is a positive outcome and hopefully it's an early sign of good things to come.[94] However, as outlined in Chapter 3, Australia's international ranking on innovation is not so good.

Ways of Thinking about Innovation

There are multiple ways of thinking about innovation. For example:

- **Work system innovations** that can make our businesses more productive.

  Productivity is a topic which is often raised in the context of Australia's business performance. The 2018 Australia Benchmark Report highlighted that "The productivity levels of 15 out of 20 Australian industries rate above the average productivity of global competitors

93 https://www.industry.gov.au/news-media/innovation-and-science-australia-news/isa-work-needed-to-improve-australias-innovation-science-and-research-system

94 https://www.westpac.com.au/content/dam/public/wbc/documents/pdf/bb/Emerging-Industries-Smart-Industry-Report.pdf

in the same sector."[95] *Australia is performing 20 per cent above this global average in five key growth sectors – gas, education, oil, tourism and health – and more than 40 per cent above in mining and agribusiness.*

This is a great result, but now is not the time to be complacent. In terms of productivity levels, we are globally competitive – however it is incumbent on business to lift its game in the innovation space.

- **Product innovation (incremental or new)** that leads to the development of better goods and services that will be demanded by people and/or businesses here and overseas. It can create new markets and/or expand existing ones.

  I have already highlighted many of the innovative products and technologies which have been developed in Australia, as well as our failure to build industries of scale that genuinely create wealth and prosperity. For example, Australia has a leading edge in medical research and biotechnology, but our capacity to commercialise in Australia is limited. ResMed and Cochlear are successful examples. CSL is another, but it is a privatised government entity.

  On the other hand, Cook Medical is an outstanding example of an international company commercialising Australian medical innovation. Cook Australia is based in Brisbane and began a division to develop, manufacture and distribute programmable pumps and infusion devices outside the United States.

- **Business model innovation (incremental or new)** that can help businesses to compete successfully both locally and internationally. Uber and AirBnb are two companies that have disrupted industries throughout thought the world with new/different business models.

  This type of innovation is exponentially more difficult to do. However, if Australian entrepreneurs can lead the world (like the Atlassian, Aconex and Canva unicorns have demonstrated), then surely, we have the capacity for business model innovation too?

95 https://www.austrade.gov.au/international/invest/resources/benchmark-report-2018/charts/charts

- **Talking about Innovation in Australia**

  Conversations about innovation aren't new in Australia, even though they may have failed to resonate with the general public. Innovation has been on our agenda for a long time. The Australian Government has commissioned over 60 reports on innovation and related areas in the past fifteen years.[96] *The Rudd Government commissioned a series of Australian Innovation Systems reports that were produced between 2010 and 2017 by the Department of Industry, Innovation and Science as a commentary on the state of innovation in Australia.*[97]

The reports were themed each year, as highlighted in the following table.

Year	Theme
2017	The impact of innovation on business, industry and national performance
2016	The evolution of Australia's indicators
2015	Innovative entrepreneurship
2014	Innovation-driven competitiveness
2013	The Asian century
2012	Innovation and productivity
2011	The underpinnings of innovation
2010	A compendium of innovation indicators

96 https://theconversation.com/australias-innovation-problem-explained-in-10-charts-51898

97 https://www.industry.gov.au/data-and-publications/australian-innovation-system-report

But even though these reports were produced each year for eight years, who read them? Probably only the people below:

- those who wrote them
- ministerial advisers (and maybe advisers to Federal Opposition?) journalists looking for a 'news story' for the day
- academics
- corporates looking for government funding.

It's indictable really. I've read parts of them all and they are a source of valuable information. But they get little or no media or business traction. In some ways it reflects Australia's innovation story – apathy and ignorance – a not- so-great story about our future.

For example, the 2016 report on Australia's indicators compared to the rest of the world reveals that:

- the adoption of innovations developed by others is the most common type of innovation in Australian businesses.
- Australia earns only a relatively modest proportion of its total income from sales of innovative products and services compared to other OECD countries.

The findings are consistent with a recent Boston Consulting Group report on *The 50 Most Innovative Companies in the World*. It's no surprise that not one Australian company is on the list.[98]

But did you know that the Australian Government injects $9.7 billion each year on research and development for science and innovation?[99] That's right, nearly $10 BILLION each year. That figure is really impressive. There are many outcomes but not all of them are visible. What are the tangible commercial outcomes of that investment other than creating jobs for scientists in universities?

98 https://www.bcg.com/publications/collections/most-innovative-companies-2018.aspx
99 https://www.smartcompany.com.au/startupsmart/advice/startupsmart-growth/startupsmart-innovation/australia-spends-10-billion-a-year-on-research-and-development-so-wheres-all-the-innovation/

This 'research and innovation' funding is spread across 13 portfolios and 150 budget line items. And despite all this funding, in 2015 Professor Roy Green (Chair of the UTS Innovation Council) highlighted that:

1. Australia's regional neighbours innovate far better than us.
2. Australia's pivot to a digital economy has stalled.
3. Australia's venture capital market has not recovered.
4. Australia has done little in the past 10 years to lower barriers to entrepreneurship.
5. Australian businesses lack a high-performance innovation culture.
6. Australia's companies are not global in nature.
7. Australia's government support for innovation favours big business over small.
8. Australian government funding for research and development has been heavily focused on tax incentives.
9. Australia performs poorly on collaboration between the business and research sectors.[100]

That was in 2015. Has anything changed?

I pointed out in Chapter 3 that only 30 per cent of Australia's research and development workforce is employed in industry, whereas this figure is closer to 80 per cent in advanced economies such as the US. Australia rates poorly internationally in terms of industry-led innovation. That fact, combined with the lack of corporate headquarters mentioned earlier, might be a major reason for the problem.

Given the time energy and money which has been spent, you can be forgiven for expecting that Australia would have a reasonable grasp of the innovation territory. We should be flooded with jobs created from this research. Where are they? While I have previously mentioned UniQuest's record of start-up creation, I still believe that a fundamental question to be answered is: what 'for profit' companies are being created in Australia?

100 https://theconversation.com/australias-innovation-problem-explained-in-10-charts-51898

Malcolm Turnbull's attempt to put the innovation agenda front and centre in the Australian conversation ultimately failed. All that it really did was open up a plethora of opportunities for consultants, educators and bloggers.

This agenda was doomed from the start. Redoubling our efforts in similar directions is futile. What are our options? There are countries in the world who in recent decades have moved in leaps and bounds. What are we learning from them?

A highly innovative and competitive business sector is the one chance we have of building an inclusive and prosperous society in the future. The prize for getting it right is a bigger share of global wealth, more (and better jobs), and better products and services to address Australia's challenges.

A Canary Chirp or a Kookaburra Crying?

The Australian government set up the Innovation and Science Australia (ISA) Board in 2016. It's made up of 15 entrepreneurs, investors and educators with both local and international experience. The ISA subsequently produced a report *Australia 2030: Prosperity through Innovation*. In the foreword to that report, ISA chair Bill Ferris lamented that Australia is "*falling behind our global peers, particularly in student performance in science and mathematics, and in business investment in research and development. This is more than a canary chirp in our economic mineshaft: it is a clarion call for national action.*"[101]

As a nation we have so far been unable to have a positive conversation about a subject which is the substance of our future – our capacity to be a prosperous nation. Investment in innovation is a great concept only if we have:

- a vibrant business community focused on something other than the next quarterly result and
- politicians who have both the will and the skill to rise above ideological claptrap and contribute to a great debate about our future.

Unfortunately, we don't have either of these essential elements at the moment.

101 https://www.industry.gov.au/sites/g/files/net3906/f/May%202018/document/pdf/australia-2030-prosperity-through-innovation-full-report.pdf

If you don't accept that, consider the industry debates over the last 10 years. The car industry, banking, mining, and energy come to mind. The themes of those debates are summarised below:

- the car industry – its demise.
- the banking sector – less than ethical behaviour.
- mining and energy – It's the 21st century and Australia is having third world challenges providing a power system for ourselves. Why is it happening? Is it the debate about the environment with the renewables versus coal divide, or is it from a lack of imagination and lack of will?

Now think of the conversations about social issues (marriage and gender issues, immigration, and the 'pass the parcel' Prime Ministerial leadership struggles) over the same period that have consumed months and years of time.

Few of the industry debates we've had have been positive either. We've seen the withdrawal of major players and the demise of the car industry. The Financial Services Royal Commission has exposed regulatory failure, greed and incompetence. It has also claimed scalps and made many recommendations which are likely to lead to necessary reform in that sector to counteract unethical and illegal behaviour. However, these reforms are unlikely to create any future wealth.

Then there's the mining and energy industry debate, with moves by a few to deconstruct the coal industry of the future. Surely, we can be more creative. Australian prosperity has been built on our natural resources and our mining industry has been a major contributor. It is one area where we're among the world leaders.[102] It is a major driver in our economy and yet there are 'interests' in Australia that would close it down. There are very few thinking people in the world who are not concerned about fossil fuels and their impact – but closing down whole industries is not a viable solution.

The ongoing energy debate highlights genuine failures in government planning over many years. We appear to be unable to supply our own needs. Yet Australia has a massive natural resource base which cannot be left underdeveloped. We have some of the largest deposits of minerals

102 https://www.austrade.gov.au/International/Invest/Resources/Benchmark-Report

in the world. Uranium, brown and black coal, and gas are energy sources. In addition, our emerging renewable energy industry – wind, hydro and solar to name a few – puts us in a position where we have an obligation to develop these resources for communities beyond Australia.

There are many countries in the world who are 'energy disadvantaged'. If we do nothing, they might do something instead. So why aren't we having a major debate about battery storage and supplying the world (our neighbours) with clean energy? It comes back to lack of foresight, a lack of political courage, complacency or incompetence.

Of course, it is a challenging problem but solving challenging problems is also a major market/business opportunity. It may even be a major wealth creation opportunity for Australia. Imagine the possibilities.

The focus of many industry conversations is often acrimonious and wealth-limiting, self-interested or about generically 'poor' government policy. These conversations are about government expenditure or wealth redistribution, rather than the creation of wealth which actually contributes to national prosperity.

In my view, the summary of all of these issues sounds more like a kookaburra crying than a canary chirp. There is so much possibility.

The sub-title of the *Australia 2030* ISA report (*Prosperity through Innovation*) is right on the money. Innovation in a vacuum is meaningless. As I pointed out in Chapter 3, Australia needs a national vision – a story that galvanises us all. Instead, the public arena conversation on a good day is currently about the economy, debts and deficits, creating jobs and tax reform. All of these discussions are good and need to be had, but they are means, not ends.

It's a little like working in a business and talking about cutting costs, managing balance sheets, profit and loss statements and tax minimisation – all legitimate topics, but none of them actually take you anywhere or create any sense of direction or hope.

Innovation is still only a means to an end. It is urgent that each of our industries forms a view about Australia's place in the world and the difference we can make. Courageous leadership is required.

The ISA report outlines five innovation imperatives:

1. Education
2. Industry
3. Government
4. Research and Development
5. Culture and Ambition.

The report makes a combined total of 30 recommendations under these five imperatives. Recommendations 27 and 28 are as follows.

> *"27) Establish a National Mission to help make Australia the healthiest nation on earth, with a step-change investment in our national genomics and personalised medicine capability and its integration into our medical research and healthcare system." (This is a positive national statement.)*
>
> *"28) Adopt a framework to continue to identify and implement National Missions." (This is a process statement).*

Who can argue with a National Health Mission (27)? The next recommendation – what does it mean and who will do it? However, it does open up the possibility of creating some national or even industry debate about future projects.

The report also suggests two potential 'National Mission' candidates:

1. *Restore the Reef: Preserving the Great Barrier Reef beyond 2030.*
2. *Hydrogen City – this potential Mission would lay the groundwork for the de-carbonisation of the direct combustion sector, which is currently responsible for 18 per cent of Australia's greenhouse gas emissions, by converting the gas supply of an entire Australian city from natural gas to clean hydrogen."*

It's disappointing that the report didn't go further and propose more 'moon shots' that Australians could aspire to and/or debate for an extended period. I'll talk more about possible 'moon shots' in Chapter 10.

Malcolm Turnbull later announced funding to help Australia become one of the top 10 defence manufacturing exporters in the world (we're currently 20th).[103]

103 https://www.sbs.com.au/news/defence-exports-turnbull-unveils-3-8b-fund-to-boost-foreign-sales-of-australian-arms

That's another positive national statement. However, I imagine this report will go the way of all the others – into the great 'library' of innovation reports in the sky.

Australia's Tech Future

Technology undoubtedly plays a significant role in what is an exciting time in the innovation world. Just look at some of the technological developments of recent times:

- 3D printing
- nanotechnology
- space technologies
- energy capture and storage technologies
- biotechnologies
- artificial intelligence and robotics
- neurotechnologies
- virtual and augmented realities
- ubiquitous sensors
- blockchain/distributed ledgers.

These are just a few. More are emerging as we speak.

Robert Friedman highlighted 2007 as a pivotal year in the technology revolution in *Thank You for Being Late*, naming over 20 technology breakthroughs (starting with the iPhone) just in that year alone.[104]

Australia needs to lead the world in capitalising on the potential of technologies like these. Every industry, from farming to aerospace, healthcare to education is likely to continue to be profoundly affected by technology. The changes are emerging at a bewildering rate.

In late 2018, the Australian government launched its digital strategy in a report titled *Australia's Tech Future*. The strategy aims to maximise Australia's opportunities for capitalising on technology by focusing on four key areas:

104 https://www.goodreads.com/book/show/26114127-thank-you-for-being-late

1. people: developing Australia's digital skills and leaving no one behind
2. services: how government can better deliver digital services
3. digital assets: building infrastructure and providing secure access to high-quality data
4. the enabling environment: maintaining our cyber security and reviewing our regulatory systems.[105]

I believe that the government's priority should be to position Australia as a leading nation in the research development and exploitation of artificial intelligence and machine learning across the digital economy. This is one of the technology areas identified in the *Australia's Tech Future* report, along with blockchain, the Internet of Things (IoT) and quantum computing. However, the report also identified that Australia currently has a skills shortage in the following areas:

- data management and analysis
- cyber security
- cloud computing
- artificial intelligence and machine learning
- robotics
- digital design
- software design
- advanced mathematics and statistics

One gem in the report was a statement that Australia is leading the development of new international standards for blockchain technologies. Another is a report by Data61 estimating that improvements to existing industries and the growth of new ones could be worth $315 billion to the Australian economy over the next decade.

However, this is a report on Australia's technological future. We are living through one of history's great technology revolutions. At a global level it

105 https://www.industry.gov.au/strategies-for-the-future/participating-in-the-digital-economy

is being described as 'Industry 4.0', yet that is not even mentioned in the report.

The vision articulated is vague:

"That Australians enjoy an enhanced quality of life and share in the opportunities of a growing, globally competitive modern economy, enabled by technology."[106]

Key Points

- 8 Innovation System Reports were published (2010 – 2017).
- The Australia 2030 – Prosperity through Innovation report was published in 2018 and identified the concept of a National Mission to *"help make Australia the healthiest nation on earth, with a step-change investment in our national genomics and personalised medicine capability and its integration into our medical research and healthcare system."*

106 https://www.industry.gov.au/data-and-publications/australias-tech-future

PART THREE

Australia's Challenges in a Rapidly Globalising World

Chapter 5
CHANGE, INNOVATION AND DISRUPTION

"The quickest way to find out who your enemies are is to try doing something new."

—Carl Gustav Jung[107]

Introduction

This chapter looks at a major obstacle to innovation in Australia – resistance to change and fear of failure. Change, innovation and disruption are words that are now 'de rigueur' in any political or business conversation. But they have been constants throughout human history, even though we seem to believe that they are modern phenomena.

Our capacity to resist change is limitless and it is not always rational. Phrases like "too hard", "not necessary", and "the existing system is fine" roll off the tongue with ease. Less visible but no less powerful include "not invented here" or "not my idea". Over many years working as a 'change agent' with more than 250 CEOs, I can say many have pointed out to me that the trick is to get them to think it's their idea. What a surprise.

As a species we are hard wired to seek comfort and ease – the choice to change is hard.

Resistance to Change

In Chapter 1, I said that starting innovative entrepreneurial businesses is simply not in Australia's DNA. The reasons are many and risk avoidance (which implicitly involves the need to change) might be one. Any innovation inevitably involves some degree of change.

Creating an entrepreneurial business is a major change – certainly for the entrepreneur and probably for the market. For many it involves putting your life/livelihood on the line. Many entrepreneurs that I've worked with have had mortgages on their homes for years as they worked through the

107 Introduction: Innovation and its enemies – Why People resist New Technologies, Calestous Juma, Oxford University Press, 2016.

start-up phase. Some have in fact lost their homes because their ventures did not go as well as they had hoped. These are major risks and profound changes.

Only recently when reviewing some old theatre programs left by my mother, I found an advertisement selling electricity in the 1930s. It's hard to consider something as ubiquitous as electricity as a change. Wood stoves, kerosene lanterns – it was a major change. Dare I say some resisted it.

"The time will come when every housewife will cook with electricity because it is simple, efficient, and economical......" [108]

Just imagine having to market electricity.

Dieting is a simple example of change in everyday life. For most people, dieting is a 'change by personal choice'. Only small changes in their lifestyle are required. But a whole industry has been established to support those who wish to lose weight.

Resistance to change is a personal choice. I actually avoided using computers for 24 years. I was what's called a 'laggard' in new product adoption terms. Although I was first introduced to computers in 1971, there was a 'typing pool' back then to do all documentation work for me. I graduated to having my own personal assistant (PA). It took self-employment in 1991 for me to buy my first computer. After a couple of years, my wife Sally announced that I had to learn to do all documentation work for myself. I had to bite the bullet. It wasn't easy for me to learn to use a computer effectively (mastery is a long way off. But I am learning.). The difference now, is I'm committed to using the technology.

It is easier to accept changes where we can see immediate benefits, even if we passively or actively resist it to start with. Innovations that we choose to adopt (i.e. that aren't imposed on us) still take time and a period of adjustment.

When change is outside of our control (i.e. imposed) there is a range of emotions – anger, fear, disillusionment and frustration. These are very powerful emotions and they limit our capacity to see the positive aspects of the change.

108 Wintergarden theatre programs 1937

For example, my parents grew up in a time of huge turbulence and disruption which I think makes what we're living through now look like a walk in the park. The changes, innovations and disruptions in that era were dramatic. Not only did they experience World War I, the Great Depression and World War II, they also lived through an era where innovations like electricity, the telephone, refrigeration, radio, television, cars, and air travel all became a reality. Each one of these innovations was disruptive in its own way and they experienced their own initial resistance in the consumer adoption cycle.

It's important to understand that while all innovations generally involve change, not all innovations are disruptive.

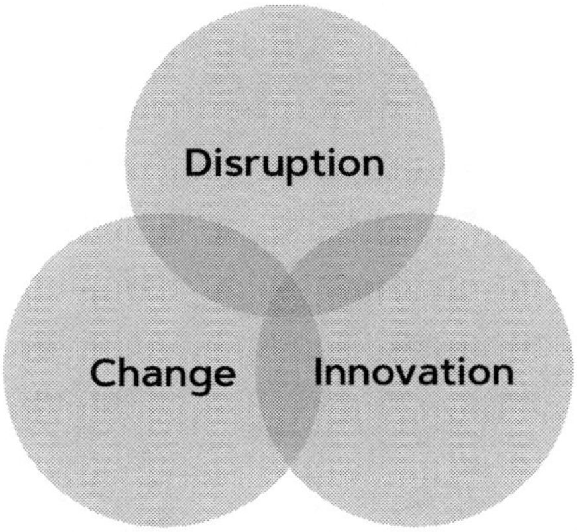

In his book *The Innovator's Dilemma,* Harvard University academic Clay Christensen outlines that disruptive innovation focuses on technology to create new markets, value networks and industries. Market leaders and entire industries are challenged and displaced when disruptive innovation occurs.[109]

It's been happening throughout human history. For example:

- cars replaced horses
- refrigeration replaced blocks of ice
- air travel was initially a revolutionary new concept.

109 https://www.amazon.com/Innovators-Dilemma-Revolutionary-Change-Business/dp/0062060244

- recently, companies like Uber and Airbnb have disrupted the taxi and accommodation industries around the world.

Incremental innovations on the other hand are less than revolutionary and involve improvements or upgrades to existing products, services, business processes or methods.

There are two ways of looking at profound changes. We can choose to be fearful (a victim) or we can choose to anticipate and embrace it (an adventurer).

The nature of disruptive innovation is such that people and existing players in the market often have little or no control over the changes that are happening. This causes a sense of being out of control. It creates uncertainly, fear and a sense of loss. People don't want that. It's at odds with our underlying human needs for stability, security and comfort.

Disruptive innovations often require radical learning and behavioural changes. They can also cause changes in lifestyle. For some people, their jobs and livelihoods (and even their identities) are at risk when disruptive innovation occurs in their industry. In my own life I've struggled with different changes and in my work as a consultant I have journeyed with individuals, groups and organisations to help them manage change. I've seen leaders make decisions and take actions that required great foresight and great courage. Major disruption or change is not easy for anyone at any level.

Major market players don't want disruptive innovation because it displaces them. And driving innovation as an existing market player to maintain a competitive edge can be difficult. Getting new products through 'the existing system' or introducing new technology are real challenges. Internal systemic cultural change is often near impossible to achieve.

The notion that it is somehow possible to introduce innovation into the DNA of an established business is a fantasy without radical shifts in leadership/staff behaviour and resource allocation. Remember that DNA is built-in at birth, and that includes organisational DNA. It means changing (at a core level):

- how decisions are made (especially resource allocation)
- how people are rewarded

- how the business (and the people in it) view the future
- how the business is structured
- how information is shared
- how learning is viewed.

To give you an idea about how important innovation is to business survival, it's worth comparing the Fortune 500 lists of the top 500 revenue-earning US companies over the last 50 years.[110] Only 60 companies that were on the list in 1955 still exist. That's just 12%. The other 88% have gone out of business, merged with other entities, or fallen out of the list because their revenue hasn't kept up the pace.

Who Would Innovate in Australia?

Even if we overcome innovation obstacles like the lack of entrepreneurial DNA in Australia and the general human resistance to change, an additional obstacle remains. In Chapter 3, I made the claim that Australia has become a nation of hypercritical cynics. Why would anyone want to be innovative (and run the risk of failure) in a culture like this?

This was amply demonstrated during the last Australian census. You may recall that the government introduced a major innovation at that time – the optional opportunity to complete the census questions online rather than using the traditional 'pen and paper' method.

As it happened, it did not go as well as was hoped. There were some unwanted interventions and the system was closed down for a short period until its integrity could be guaranteed. Some Australians were inconvenienced for a short time. There were some clumsy explanations about what had gone wrong, but the integrity of the system was maintained.

The response was predictable and amazing. There was much wailing and gnashing of teeth by both the informed and the uninformed. Words like catastrophe, embarrassment and disaster were bandied about. There were calls for the government to take responsibility and for heads to roll. There was a queue of commentators a mile long wanting to add condemnation.

110 http://www.aei.org/publication/fortune-500-firms-1955-v-2017-only-12-remain-thanks-to-the-creative-destruction-that-fuels-economic-prosperity/

The venom and the vitriol levelled at the Australian Bureau of Statistics and their leaders (and by default, the government) was amazing.[111]

Many of those making the comments have never introduced a major change in their lives and have no concept of the magnitude and complexity of the task. They are happy from their voyeuristic seats to criticise, carp and condemn people who are out there doing the work (innovating).

The collection of online data for the census was a major innovation and there was a glitch. But there has never been a major innovation that didn't have problems. It doesn't mean that the whole system is flawed or that those involved in its development and delivery are deserving of proverbial public 'floggings'. It means there are huge opportunities for learning and maybe real savings over time.

Unfortunately, it's likely that the concept of online elections (and all the cost savings that would entail) has been derailed for at least another generation due to this online census hiccup and the public response.

If this is how Australia reacts to future innovation attempts, then we have no hope.

The NBN is another contemporary example. It's the first substantive nation-building project we've done for decades, but it's plagued by gnawing criticism on both sides. Is there a reason (apart from small-minded political point-scoring) why the political parties could not come together and agree on a 'moon shot' around technological competence in Australia? The *Australia's Tech Future* document highlighted in Chapter 4 is another missed opportunity.

It appears that any major or minor project in Australia is faced with major resistance, critique and an 'if I didn't think of it, it must be 'bad' mentality. However, innovation requires courage on one hand and a social capacity for resilience on the other.

There is a case to argue that we lack imagination, foresight, and courage. Is it any wonder that our governments are reluctant to make major changes? We are very comfortable to wallow in our 'lucky lifestyle'.

111 https://www.theguardian.com/australia-news/2016/aug/10/computer-says-no-australian-census-shambles-explanation-depends-on-who-you-ask

It doesn't matter what government is in power, Australians are generally 'critics' and 'naysayers' of the highest order with very little positive to say and very few solutions. Instead, many simply expect/demand the government to fix our problems. Then if they act, we rise against it. Maybe it's our convict mentality. I remember my grandfather saying, "Australians are instinctively 'agin' the government."

There has been little to no genuine structural reform of the economy since the introduction of the GST in 2000. After 28 years of economic growth, it's fair to say we are in a flat spot.

One commentator even suggested in relation to the obsession with short-term opinion polls and our revolving door of Prime Ministers in recent years, that *"perhaps the problem isn't with the office holder, but with us and the lifestyle we expect to lead."*[112] I believe that sentiment can be applied to innovation more broadly.

The ideas of innovation change and disruption do not sit easily in a political context. In the 1980s and 1990s when economic and structural reform were actually the agenda – what was different?

Paul Keating offered an insight in his memorial address at Bob Hawke's funeral: *"At the core of it, Bob and I shared one primary idea: that Australia's creativity had been locked down by a stultifying paternal policy regimen …." He also highlighted the three key elements of "policy creativity, coherence and continuity".*[113]

The economic and structural reform of that time is considered as the platform for our current period of prosperity. What is the platform for prosperity for our grandchildren?

What if the Business Council of Australia and other leading industry bodies set up a fund to develop the sorts of nation-building innovations that they believe Australia needs over the next 50 years?

112 https://www.theaustralian.com.au/life/weekend-australian-magazine/abbotts-been-thrown-to-the-dogs/news-story/0358956728cc0a296cfe8515bb90a4be

113 https://www.theaustralian.com.au/nation/trust-held-me-and-bob-together-paul-keatings-eulogy-to-bob-hawke/news-story/4da3e8208ec10fe6d782083fdcf0d66c

After all, business is the dominant institution in our society. Perhaps it's time for the business sector to take responsibility for more than just itself and the payment of outrageous salaries to its executives and directors. They're all keen to demonstrate social responsibility, so wouldn't building Australia's long-term future prosperity be the ultimate social program?

Instead, business seems to be blinded by generating short-term shareholder value, and governments are hamstrung by short-term opinion polls and cheap point-scoring over their political opponents.

At the very least, perhaps the business sector and the Australian government could agree on some major priorities. They could agree on 10–15 nation-building 'moon shots' that would have bipartisan support and help to ensure our long-term national prosperity. The projects could be implemented over a 30-year timeframe, one per election term, regardless of which political party was in power.

The current political situation where the major stakeholders throw hand grenades at each other every time a major innovation is proposed isn't acceptable. What's even worse is an incoming government dismantling a project after it has started because they didn't support it in the first place. That's such a waste of time, money and energy.

Key Points

- Irrational resistance to change is a major obstacle to innovation.
- What if the Business Council of Australia and other leading industry bodies set up a fund to develop the sorts of nation-building innovations that they believe Australia needs over the next 50 years?

Chapter 6
THE CHALLENGE

"Serious people laughed at me when I told them I wanted to build a telecommunications network in Africa twenty years ago."

—Mo Ibrahim[114]

Introduction

This chapter looks at the challenge being posed by the Fourth Industrial Revolution that we are experiencing globally, and the urgent need for Australia to position itself to capitalise on it. It also analyses how we're currently responding.

The Fourth Industrial Revolution

The Fourth Industrial Revolution is shaking the world and disrupting entire industries. It's being led by technology. The nature of work is changing and the whole system of employment relationships is being restructured.

- The First Industrial Revolution introduced mechanisation, water and steam power.
- The Second introduced electric power to create mass production.
- The Third introduced electronics and information technology to automate production.
- The Fourth Industrial Revolution is building on the Third. It is a digital revolution that has been occurring since the middle of the last century. It's characterised by a fusion of technologies that is blurring the lines between the physical, digital, and biological spheres.

Contemporary disruption is predominantly digital and it's happening rapidly. For example:

- the world's largest taxi company owns no taxis (Uber).

114 https://www.goodreads.com/en/book/show/37868583-the-prosperity-paradox

- the world's largest accommodation provider owns no properties (Airbnb).
- the world's largest phone companies own no telecommunications infrastructure (Skype and WeChat).
- the world's most valuable retailer has no inventory (Alibaba).
- the world's most popular media owner creates no content (Facebook).
- the world's largest movie house owns no cinemas (Netflix).[115]

In many cases these disruptors are already at work in our business world and some industries are just not prepared (e.g. taxis). In any major disruption there are winners and losers. No change occurs without major costs – social and economic.

I suspect there are those from the previous three revolutions who considered their changes radical and transformative by their generational standards. Just imagine people transitioning from agricultural to industrial work (or just automating their basic farm work.) The work in factories was often done in less than optimum conditions and skills were a limited consideration. Now we are concerned that over-educated young people have work that is not commensurate with their educational levels. My suspicion is that this is a first- world problem.

My baby boomer generation has lived through a period of unprecedented global stability and economic growth. Australia has achieved economic growth each year since 1991. This is a major achievement. I have suggested earlier that the period of economic restructuring in the 1980s and 1990s was the platform for this. However, CEO of Freelancer Matt Barrie has a more confronting view, suggesting in 2017 that:

"Australia is a property bubble floating inside a mining bubble inside a commodities bubble inside a China bubble and that lucky free ride is about to go pop."[116]

Whatever the source of growth, there is little evidence that human systems can sustain these high levels of performance for extended periods of time.

115 https://twitter.com/mysocietyone/status/667602245488275456
116 https://medium.com/@matt_11659/matt-barrie-australias-economy-is-a-house-of-cards-6877adb3fb2f

I have referred to my parents' generation earlier. They lived through World War I, the Great Depression and World War II. All of these events were profoundly disruptive in their own way. For many young Australian men of that era, their first job was joining the Armed Forces to fight in World War II. For women there also were changes – working in factories, on farms and more widely across the work environment to replace the men and to make their War contribution. It was a collective effort. After the Wars, the women returned to their homes to support their families. It was a profoundly disruptive time for both men and women. While we may argue that the disruption we face today is faster, bigger and more systemic, I know which generational disruption I'd prefer.

A recent report by the Foundation for Young Australians (FYA) revealed that young people today are more educated than ever, with 60 per cent holding post-school qualifications. But the report also revealed that 50 per cent of our young adults aged under 25 weren't able to find full-time work in their chosen field after finishing their studies.[117]

FYA Chief Executive Jan Owen made the following comment when releasing the report:

"Australia's promise to our young people has been that their education is the 'golden ticket' to a full-time job. Over the past decade however, that promise to the next generation has been broken as Australia is failing to stay responsive and relevant in a rapidly changing world."[118]

STEM

Australia has invested in education as a platform for increasing the prosperity of the nation for decades. In the late 1960s, only 5-10% of young Australians received a tertiary education. Now it's closer to 40%.

The growth in our economy is currently driven by the service sector, and it employs nearly 80 per cent of Australians.[119] There is now a major call for

117 https://www.fya.org.au/report/the-new-work-reality/

118 https://www.news.com.au/finance/work/careers/study-reveals-the-struggle-of-young-australians-to-find-fulltime-work/news-story/f1137a1fbf16fee2769ea1b5deceb211

119 https://publications.industry.gov.au/publications/industryinsightsjune2018/documents/IndustryInsights_1_2018_ONLINE.pdf

STEM (science, technology, engineering and mathematics) to receive a much greater focus in the education system and for many more students to engage with these subjects.[120] That suggests we want our young Australians to work in technology-focused industries or universities in the future. It begs the following questions:

1. What is it about STEM that is going to create prosperity for Australia?
2. What are the future industries with jobs for young Australians who have STEM skills when 80% of our jobs are currently in service Industries?

The government is attempting to answer these questions by funding six growth centres with the stated aim of driving Australia's innovation, productivity and competitiveness.[121] The six sectors are:

- Advanced Manufacturing
- Cyber Security
- Food and Agribusiness
- Medical Technologies and Pharmaceuticals
- Mining Equipment, Technology and Services
- Oil, Gas and Energy Resources.

But do you ever hear much about these growth centres or what they're doing? If these industries are the platform for our prosperity, their profile in public discussion is almost non-existent (with the exception of mining, which gets a regular 'green flogging'). Why is that? Is there nothing to celebrate? Is there something about the future which is undiscussable?

However, each sector has published a vision as part of their sector competitiveness plan. These visions are outlined below. What is required now is a national conversation about each vision.

120 https://www.smh.com.au/education/australia-s-education-system-needs-transforming-20190115-p50ri6.html
121 https://www.industry.gov.au/strategies-for-the-future/growth-centres

Sector Visions

Advanced Manufacturing

To develop an internationally competitive, dynamic and thriving Australian advanced manufacturing sector that boosts the long-term health of the economy and the nation.

Cyber Security

To strengthen Australia's cybersecurity ecosystem and help Australia become a powerful cybersecurity exporter and world-leading cybersecurity education hub.

Food and Agribusiness

By 2025, the industry is working together to grow the share of Australian food in the global marketplace.

Medical Technologies and Pharmaceuticals

For Australia to retain all current and planned levels of R&D expenditure while achieving greater commercialisation success, creating more products that reach proof-of-concept and early-stage commercialisation, increasing the number of medium to large companies with late-stage product successes, and maximising the value of any IP monetisation events along the way. The overall effect would be greater employment and wealth creation for Australia.

Mining Equipment, Technology and Services (METS)

The vision for METS is an industry-aligned, collaborative and agile ecosystem and, through leadership and innovation, growing share of the global market.

Oil, Gas and Energy Resources

To maximise the value to the Australian economy by having an energy resources sector which is globally competitive, growing, sustainable, innovative and diverse.

Much time and energy has been devoted to the development of these sector competitiveness plans and visions, but who knows about them? One can only assume there was a high level of participation by business leaders and other industry players. If not, this work will fade away into the vast cavern of papers and reports which amount to nothing.

The visions could be much clearer and have more focus – there is little 'land a person on the Moon' stimulus – but they are a start. Link these together with the work CSIRO has done (outlined in Chapter 3) and there is an emerging narrative.

All of these documents need more 'airtime', both within industries and within the education system. I suspect there are very few schools and universities that have these industry visions (or the *Innovation System Reports*) as a part of their curriculum.

One of the big questions for Australia is:

How do we create a society that is open and willing to learn and adapt in a world where accelerating changes (social and technological) are continuing and radical?

Lifelong Learning

Lifelong learning is not a new concept but the application of it is. For many, learning is something that happens at school or in a classroom. In reality, learning really occurs for adults in times of:

- life crises – for example, the death of a loved one, business failure or job loss.
- self-initiated projects – for example, building a home or a family, or learning a new skill.

I had the opportunity of working with educator Malcolm Knowles (author of *The Adult Learner: A Neglected Species*)[122] in the early 1980s. He told me a story about some research he was doing into how adults learnt. In summary, the research team sent out a questionnaire to a number of adults asking what they had learnt in the last 12 months. The answers came back indicating that most had learnt nothing.

This was a real surprise and the research team didn't believe it. On further examination they discovered that most people associated learning with going to a school or a course. When asked what new projects they had undertaken and what was learnt, they got a very different result. One conclusion was that adults learn from solving problems. It is project focused. Knowles pioneered the concept of andragogy (adult learning).

122 https://www.goodreads.com/book/show/132549.The_Adult_Learner

It may be that we have to consider different, more radical learning processes as we move into this technological era. Much of the actual information we need is instantly accessible on the internet via YouTube, MOOCs and other channels.

I believe that learning forums need to be established (if they're not already in place) to catalyse new learning. There have been some good examples we can learn from:

- The Prices and Incomes Accord in the 1980s and early 1990s
- The Australia 2020 Summit convened by Kevin Rudd in 2008
- The Global Food Forum most recently held in Australia in March 2019 to discuss issues facing Australia's agribusiness sector.

Each of these forums was obviously driven by different imperatives and had very different outcomes, but in exploring the questions about lifelong learning and how communities can prepare themselves for change more quickly, forums like these must be considered as an option. Dismissing them as "talk fests" displays a level of general cynicism and social critique at which Australians are distinguished. Why not lead the world at the development of forums which build social consensus? In our early history we were considered a "social laboratory". Why not now? I have already mentioned a Prosperity Commission – why not Industry Learning Forums?

Maybe the question for us now is: How do we become a learning nation? (A country that creates prosperity by learning together.) I am confident there are worse ideas.

Something must change if we are to create a more prosperous nation. These types of learning forums just might provide an early sign on a way forward. With practice and discipline, they might become a way to generate a shared view of the future. Creating a learning culture which is open to the radical changes already happening is an important step.

The design principle for these learning forums needs to be consistent with what the famous 20th century American physicist David Bohm so aptly described in his book *On Dialogue*:

"From time to time, (the) tribe gathered in a circle. They just talked and talked and talked, apparently to no purpose. They made no decisions.

There was no leader. And everybody could participate. There may have been wise men or wise women who were listened to a bit more – older ones – but everybody could talk. The meeting went on, until it finally seemed to stop for no reason at all and the group dispersed. Yet after that, everybody seemed to know what to do, because they understood each other so well. Then they could get together in smaller groups and do something or decide things."[123]

Our culture is so dominated by complacency, shortsightedness, dependence and the need to critique, we find it hard to take responsibility for our own learning. Our instinct is to fight for the status quo or in the event something must be done, we expect the government to do it. "What's for lunch?"

In a world where people are looking for answers to complex problems, the traditional learning processes need to be challenged – learning needs to be a self-generating/renewing process for adults and communities. In the same way leadership is evolving from a command and control paradigm. Learning is moving from teacher-centric models to learner-centred models, as outlined in Chapter 3.

Australia's innovation conversations are often 'fog-punching' exercises (lots of punching – hitting nothing). Of course, we think innovation is a good thing – who can argue with it? And there is no doubt we need more of it. But until there is a clearer focus, there will be a lot more 'fog punching'.

Our national conversations and debates (learning forums) should focus on the next 50 years (not the next 50 weeks) and the topics should include:

- industries of the future (e.g. the government's 'growth centres') – because they'll provide the keys to our future prosperity,
- the role of technology in creating economic wealth,
- Australia's place in the world as a 'Eurasian' nation,
- the nature of work and productivity,
- public infrastructure, and
- many others.

123 https://www.amazon.com/Dialogue-Routledge-Classics-76/dp/0415336414

It seems to me that we could have a series of forums in Australia articulating and creating multiple industry futures. These futures will enable us to articulate what the transition might be. One of the challenges in a major change is create a language to articulate the transitioning from A to B.

Change (transition) will only occur when people understand the dimensions of the transition. It's a major mind shift. The only shift I have heard talked about is the shift from an economy driven by a mining boom to a more diversified, services-based economy. So, what might that transition look like?

The following table is a simple framework to illustrate the required mind shift.

From	To
A country with a limited record in terms of business innovation	A leader in business and technology innovation (especially in Asia)
Having major Asian export partners	An economy that's integrated with Asia
A lifestyle-driven culture of entitlement	A culture driven by individuals and businesses making a contribution to the collective pursuit of national prosperity
The business pursuit of mediocrity – 'she'll be right mate.'	The business pursuit of shared value creation and global competitiveness. We might even be courageous and think about the difference we can make in the world.
Unions fighting to protect jobs	Businesses and unions working together to create jobs
Interminable debates about public infrastructure	Serious decisions being made about nation-building infrastructure
Lamenting that the mining boom is over (and dreaming about another one)	Industry wealth-creation debates

In recent times, instead of innovation and economic transition being the major focus of our national conversations, the big issues have been the environment and tax changes. In previous years, other topics have consumed the 'airtime': our national debt and deficit, 'turning back the boats', the marriage debate, the carbon tax and tax reform more broadly, as well as Royal Commissions into financial services, aged care, child abuse, and the unions.

While all of these issues are important, how does a major focus on them actually create wealth?

For example, the tax system is an industry in its own right, so of course those involved want to talk about it and reform it. Yet as one respected former political leader once said:

"......that for a nation to try to tax itself into prosperity is like a man standing in a bucket and trying to lift himself up by the handle."

—Winston S. Churchill[124]

Then there are the incessant and continuing leadership popularity polls, which in fact are a clumsy way of the media trying to create content for the voracious 24-hour news cycle. The media have become activists in the political process. Their polls are like a monthly election. Apart from generating more media content, what they achieve is a form of unhelpful instability. Governing well is not about short-term popularity. It is about making the best decisions, even if they are tough decisions.

Great leaders are not always the most popular, but they are respected.

So Where are the Thought Leaders?

Some years ago, I attended a lunch with colleagues and a question was posed: if you were putting together a group of people to create the plan to guide Australia through current economic challenges – who would you pick?

There were six of us and we were each allowed one nomination. We quickly came up with the first five names:

- Paul Keating,
- Malcolm Turnbull,
- Bill Kelty,

124 https://www.goodreads.com/quotes/tag/taxes

- Gail Kelly, and
- Tim Costello.

This group seemed self-evident. But after those obvious choices, the proverbial cupboard seemed bare. Many other names were thrown about, but there was no consensus. So, we left it at those five.

We reflected on the list we'd come up with and the conversation we'd had. We quickly realised that:

- this group probably had their best performance years behind them. So, where were the younger generation of leaders?
- business leaders and women weren't front and centre in our conversation.
- the group reflected the age of the members at the lunch.

Ironically, all of the people at the lunch were business leaders (in the later stages of their careers).

There is a wonderful story I heard many years ago about a couple of old guys – Moses and Aaron. Leaders from another time. As the story goes Moses and Aaron were leading their people somewhere and as it turned out they were a long way ahead. Aaron says to Moses – "Moses we are way out in front, maybe we should sit down?" They thought for a while – and then sat down – and so did their people.

Maybe business leaders in Australia are sitting down as well? Has our business sector become so self-serving and inward-looking that it is unable to focus on and contribute to the conversation on national prosperity? Or does business expect government to do all the heavy lifting? It appears that both are possibilities.

There are business leaders who lead and manage competently. There are also some who seem to be attracted by the next shiny object, and then there are some who just blunder along.

Business schools have been established at undergraduate, postgraduate and vocational level at universities and colleges across Australia over the past fifty years. But are Australian businesses and their leaders performing at higher levels as a result of this business education? It is a difficult and complex question.

Australia For Sale

Some time ago I read that in Australia there were more mergers, acquisitions and business sales than there were start-ups. Whether it is true now or not, given the emergence of the start-up movement (see Crossroads; https://crossroads.startupaus.org), it set me thinking.

In Chapter 1, I mentioned some notable sales of iconic Australian businesses and brands over the past decade. Here's an expanded list from the past three decades:

- Queensland Cement and Lime (sold overseas in 1990)
- Bundaberg Sugar (1991)
- Tooheys (1992)
- Castlemaine Perkins (1992)
- UGG (1995)
- Aeroplane Jelly (1995)
- Birds Eye (1995)
- Tofts (1996)
- Arnott's (1997)
- Billy Tea (1998)
- QUF (Pauls) (1998)
- Ampol (1997)
- Speedo (1990s)
- Bundaberg Rum (2000)
- Herron (2003)
- Uncle Toby's (2006)
- Victa (2008)
- Golden Circle (2009)
- Esky (2009)
- Fosters (2011)

- Billabong (2012)
- RM Williams (2013)
- Wendy's (2014)
- Toll (2015)
- Pacific Brands (2016)
- Dulux (2019)

Even the iconic Vegemite brand was sold overseas before Bega bought it back in 2017.

I'm confident there have been many more sales that weren't as visible as the ones listed above. For example, how many more privately owned businesses have been sold offshore? In 2016, family-owned Australian seafood company Kailis Bros sold 90 per cent of its seafood processing, wholesale and export business to a Chinese conglomerate.[125] My list also doesn't include the major purchases of land and assets by overseas interests in the sugar, grain, wine, and beef-processing industries. Although it is worth noting, as I write, that Mackay Sugar has recently sold a majority stake to a German company. 'Another one bites the dust...' While the deal ensures there is a future for Mackay growers, it is the end of an era for a major industry, as highlighted by the Chairman of Canegrowers Queensland.

"We need to be candid, there is a sense of mourning, the loss of 70 per cent of equity of the company that was part of the heritage of our fathers and grandfathers." [126]

This begs three questions worth pondering.

1. Who owns and controls our major industries?
2. Does it matter?
3. Who cares?

125 https://kailisbroswebsite.com/
126 https://www.abc.net.au/news/rural/2019-08-01/mackay-sugar-sells-70pc-stake-to-german-owned-nordzucker/11369100

4. A recent study has found that 9 out of 10 of Australia's highest sales supermarket food and beverage brands are at least partly foreign-owned.[127] I keep coming back to another question – what do these foreign owners see or what can they do that is beyond us? Is it just that we are short of capital? Or

- do we lack imagination/foresight?
- are we incompetent?
- are we too committed to lifestyle?
- do we just lack the will and capability to build businesses?
- are we greedy?
- is this an inevitable consequence of the economics of globalisation?

One interesting observation is that many of Australia's food /agricultural businesses were started by grower-owned cooperatives or statutory grower systems (statutory marketing authorities). Here's a snapshot:

- GrainCorp is the product of a number of statutory marketing boards from Queensland and New South Wales.
- Bega Cheese started as a dairy suppliers' cooperative in New South Wales.
- Wesfarmers was founded as a cooperative by Western Australian farmers.
- Golden Circle began as a government fruit marketing initiative.
- I know there are many more. It highlights a different type of entrepreneurial spirit in our DNA.

Since the Australian economy was restructured in the 1980s, we have increasingly done business in a globalised world. It's important to understand though that globalisation is a step in the journey of the human race – it's not a new economic model.

127 http://www.ausfoodnews.com.au/2017/11/08/foreign-brands-with-local-production-are-most-important-to-australian-supermarket-customers.html

Australia as a country is in fact a product of globalisation. As outlined in Chapter 1, Britain had a major social problem with prison overcrowding. They needed somewhere to place prisoners. There was also the 'strategy' of expanding the British territory through land occupation. A convict settlement was established in 1788 in Port Jackson in less than optimum circumstances. More convict settlements followed. Over time, along with convicts, came free settlers. It was 'globalisation' in that era. Australia's Indigenous people experienced this as an invasion.

Globalisation in the 1700s was about the possession of land and resources. Is it any different now? It's simply a continuation of that search driven by a more powerful economic imperative. It doesn't change the fact that as Australians we need to ask serious questions as we sell our businesses offshore, especially when the rationale for the sale is 'that the shareholders have done very well'. Another question might be: what about the other stakeholders? Further questions include the following.

- What happens to our wealth-creation capacity when a business is sold offshore?
- Who really benefits?
- Is shareholder value the most important business goal?
- Given that there is research to suggest that 70 per cent of mergers and acquisitions fail – how much value is destroyed when businesses are sold offshore?[128]
- What is the social cost of a major Australian business being sold to international interests?
- Is it possible we will wake up one day and all of our major assets will be owned by businesses or indeed countries outside of Australia? (Does it matter?)

These are just a few of the questions we need to answer. I suspect there are many more.

128 https://www.business2community.com/strategy/70-mergers-acquisitions-fail-01888557

The genesis of the Australian economy was forged in the debate on free trade versus protection. Back then it was about ensuring the survival of Australia as a fledgling country. Until the 1980s both major political parties subscribed to the idea that *"the government knew best, and that Australia was best protected and nurtured as a closed economy behind policy barbed wire."*[129]

More recently, in 2015 IBIS founder Phil Ruthven posed the sale of Australia as a 'tongue in cheek' hypothesis in his newsletter.

"Whilst purely academic, it is interesting to consider what a foreign country might pay for Australia, if only because countries – or parts of them – have been sold in the past. The USA paid $US 240.0 million (in today's terms) for the Louisiana Purchase of 2.1 million square kilometres (28.0% of Australia's land mass) from France in 1803; and a similar amount for Alaska (20.0% of Australia's land mass) from Russia in 1867. Those acquisitions, nearly half of Australia's land mass, were acquired for under $US 500 million in today's terms: a steal, as they say. Australia wouldn't go for that cheap; try $50 trillion, so each family could retire with over $5 million each.

But don't float the idea, because any of several nations could afford that, and would come running with a cheque book – with the risk that a lot of Australians might say yes."[130]

If shareholder value is the dominant value in our business culture and our company directors 'pride themselves' as having done well for their shareholders, then *why wouldn't we sell Australia*? It would mean that our 'company directors' (our politicians) would be able to say, 'the shareholders have done very well.' That is the logical extension of those economic reforms. It's a shocking thought. Or not?

How Do We Respond?

There's no doubt that globalisation and technology are major influences in our business future. We have little control over the speed or the scale of

129 https://www.theaustralian.com.au/nation/trust-held-me-and-bob-together-paul-keatings-eulogy-to-bob-hawke/news-story/4da3e8208ec10fe6d782083fdcf0d66c

130 IBISWorld Where Knowledge is Power December 2015

these changes so the big question is: how do we respond?

We can slip into a defensive mindset and fight to retain Australia as an 'old world' country, or we can start to answer that big question by answering these questions:

- are we as a nation, open to a 22nd century world?
- how do we respond positively to the acceleration of globalisation, technology and the rise of the Asian economies?
- how are we positioning Australia to take advantage of the major opportunities created by these major shifts?
- what does our industry structure look like in 50 years?

Key Points

- We're currently experiencing an unprecedented level of global change.
- Many iconic Australian businesses have been sold to international investors in recent decades.
- A recent study has found that 9 out of 10 of Australia's highest selling supermarket food and beverage brands are at least partly foreign-owned.

Chapter 7

INNOVATION – A LONG, HARD (BUT NECESSARY) ROAD

"Innovation is hard. It really is. Because most people don't get it. Remember the automobile, the airplane, these were all considered toys at their introduction because they had no constituency. They were too new."

—Nolan Bushnell[131]

Introduction

I'll start this chapter with an example to illustrate just how hard it is to innovate successfully, but at the same time, just how rewarding the payoffs can be. The remainder of the chapter will focus on the roles that business and government can play in facilitating innovation in Australian industries.

Shell is a global company with operations in Australia. Since 1996, it has run its 'Game Changer' program to "*provide innovators with the financial and technical support and space they need to demonstrate the technical and commercial viability of their ideas*".[132] Over more than two decades, it has received more than 10,000 idea submissions from more than 5,000 innovators around the world.

While that number sounds impressive, only about 10 ideas a year have enough credibility to reach the proof of concept stage. That's just 4% of the total ideas submitted. Even less (about 1%) become a reality.[133]

But the ones that do are genuine 'game changers.' For example, one of the ideas that progressed to full implementation is building a floating liquid natural gas plant (FLNG). This is a massive 600,000-tonne ship (named the Prelude FLNG) that contains a fully operational liquid natural

131 https://www.brainyquote.com/quotes/nolan_bushnell_524455
132 https://www.shell.com/energy-and-innovation/innovating-together/shell-gamechanger.html
133 https://www.innovationexcellence.com/blog/2016/03/16/shell-gamechanger-the-giant-still-wants-big-ideas/?Itemid=88

gas plant. Traditionally, LNG plants are built on land. The Prelude FLNG commenced its operations off the coast of Western Australia in late 2018. It's the largest offshore floating facility ever built anywhere in the world.[134]

The Conversations We Aren't Having in Australia

Innovation is a symbolic word in many ways. It creates a sense of excitement and progress. Over the last thirty years, Australian politics has been littered with slogans conjuring up an innovative image. *"The Clever Country"*, *"The Education Revolution"*, and *"The Smart State"* (Queensland), and most recently, former Prime Minister Malcolm Turnbull's *"A More Innovative and Agile Australia"* stand out.

But innovation is not achieved via a few slogans and mountains of reports. Innovation happens when business, government and the community are able to have tough conversations and make courageous decisions. It requires foresight and courage. The bottom line is that innovation in any sphere is tough.

From my perspective of having worked in (and with) start-ups, SMEs and corporates in Australia for over 40 years, innovation is talked about (and in some cases, there are initiatives), but it is a long, hard road. Whether it is new social technologies, creating productive work cultures or introducing new management practices in the 1980s, licensing new technologies in the 1990s, or launching new products – there are no 'easy metres'. In the early planning phases I often say, "Pick a $ figure and double it, pick a time frame and double it, pick a degree of difficulty and treble it.

Innovation at any level is a challenging task. Building an innovative business is not for the faint-hearted. In a very few cases there is an individual who is gifted and can change the world through combining their capacity to innovate with timing and opportunity – Steve Jobs was one, Elon Musk is another. Timing and opportunity are critical. Steve Jobs was brilliant at design and marketing, but much of his product development was the result of years of government-funded research. *"There are 12 major technologies*

134 https://www.smh.com.au/business/companies/world-s-largest-floating-lng-platform-starts-production-in-wa-20181226-p50ob1.html

integrated within the iPod, iPhone, and iPad that stand out as features.... These breakthroughs were the result of research carried out in various public-private partnerships at labs .....a number of US research facilities." [135]

Successful innovation can happen in a variety of ways, but it occurs often when people are focused on solving a problem and/or meeting a consumer need/want (even if it's unidentified). Occasionally it happens when someone sees a pattern or a trend early and moves quickly.

Innovation conversations in Australia rarely talk about the number of ideas you need to generate to find the real 'game changers'. The Shell example at the start of this chapter highlights that reality.

Nor do you hear any discussion in Australia about the outputs of all the innovation investment that is going on. Instead, the conversation focuses on the inputs to the innovation system. And there are many of them. Just a few include:

- more government funding
- more students studying STEM
- more incubators
- more landing pads
- more engagement with Asia
- a national innovation system
- and the list goes on and on.

The *2019 Australia Benchmark Report* published the following innovation indicators:[136]

- we rank third in terms of the number of universities in the world's top 100.
- the CSIRO ranks in the top 1% of the world's scientific institutions in 14 research fields.
- 49% of Australian firms are 'innovation active'.

135 https://www.smh.com.au/business/companies/world-s-largest-floating-lng-platform-starts-production-in-wa-20181226-p50ob1.html
136 https://www.austrade.gov.au/international/invest/resources/benchmark-report-2018/charts/charts

- we are ranked 5th in terms of global entrepreneurship.
- we rank first for technology readiness. (This is a surprise given our NBN situation).

However, we are again measuring *inputs* to the innovation process. One output of innovation is prosperity.

Have we developed a number of *prosperity measures* for the 21st century to shift the debate to the outcomes of the innovation investments? If so, what are they? Certainly, neither of the major political parties are talking about them.

There is more to prosperity than GDP. Many of our global rankings are middle of the road, and for a country with our resources and talent, maybe we should be aiming higher. Where does that conversation happen? Certainly not in any public forum I am aware of. Just imagine if each year (or every three years) the government published the "Australian Prosperity Report" measuring the impact of business performance and government policy? This might be an innovative initiative in a social experiment like Australia.

There is also very little conversation about the nature of the innovation that we're expecting or demanding, nor what markets or problems we're tackling.

The data in the *2019 Australia Benchmark Report* also suggests that we are among the leaders in R&D expenditure in the world. The outcome is measured by the relative impact of Australian scientific research. While I am impressed with the data and the number and quality of the research papers produced – it does not compare with the revenue outcomes generated in the MIT example in Chapter 3.

It would be more interesting and relevant to discuss innovation as we move forward in the context of outputs and real-world impacts rather than inputs – outputs are at least focused on the product/market end of the chain, which is where the rubber meets the road. Producing another innovation statement or report creates the perception that something is happening. Australia's innovation track record suggests that it's not.

The Commercial Imperative

Innovation is a commercial imperative for businesses to create competitive advantage, maintain or grow market share, and ensure ongoing profitability.

Business innovation is multi-layered, and (as outlined in Chapter 4), it can involve:

- product innovation. For example, incremental improvements to existing products and/or the development of new products to create new markets
- business model innovation (incremental or new)
- productivity improvements via improving or developing new processes.

Obviously incremental improvements are more manageable, but to go down the track of new products, new business models and major productivity breakthroughs requires courage, commitment, money and a very long-time horizon. Maybe if our government could set a good example in all those areas it would be a good start.

Innovation questions that understandably concern businesses include:

1. how long does it take for an innovative new product to get traction in the market?

   Remember, consumers can be resistant to change and launching a new product or service is rarely an easy task. For example, in the area of medical research where we are a world leader, the time frames (product to market) are 10-20 years.

2. when will that new product be profitable?

   In some cases, getting national support in Australia or management support within a business for innovation efforts is a massive challenge. The established system inevitably has the power and has a mortgage over all the resources. Few systems embrace radical changes willingly. Organisations form habits and breaking their expenditure patterns and focus is the challenge.

I remember reading a story that Peter Drucker is reported to have told:

If you have a person in the business with a great idea – the first thing you do is take resources away. The second thing you do is take more resources away. The third thing you do is take even more resources away. If then the person is still standing – give them all the resources they need because the person who is standing is a 'mono maniac with a mission' This is what it takes to be a genuine innovator.

There is a reason the venture capital industry talks about 'The Valley of Death'. This is the time when innovations are likely to fail through lack of funds – support. It is all a function of learning and adapting – and how quickly we can do it.

The reality about innovation is that businesses that start now are 5 – 10 – 15 years away from any real return depending on the industry they're operating in and the nature of the innovation.

The Role of Government

Governments have a role to play in creating an environment for business innovation. That environment can enable business to generate wealth and create employment for the good of the nation. There is clearly a role for government in encouraging pioneering business ventures.

As I've said earlier, it's important to understand that business is the major (or perhaps the only) wealth creation institution in society. The success of business and individuals in society helps to fund the essential public services that we need governments to provide via the tax system, such as:

- defence
- education
- health
- social welfare
- and many others.

A robust, high-functioning business sector which is innovative, agile and productive, is the platform for Australia's future prosperity.

Besides creating an environment that encourages businesses to innovate, governments also have an important role to play in making investment decisions in new technologies and decisions for nation-building infrastructure. A review of the national infrastructure plan highlights a number of national projects:[137]

137 https://infrastructureaustralia.gov.au/policy-publications/publications/Australian-Infrastructure-Plan.aspx

- Transport:
  - Inland Rail (Melbourne to Brisbane)
  - Outback Way (Western Australia to Queensland)
- Communications
  - NBN
  - Jindalee Operational Radar Network Upgrade
- Energy
  - Snowy Hydro 2.0

While the existence of this national infrastructure plan is evidence that work is happening, it could be much more ambitious. Much of the plan focuses on incremental work in the states and regional Australia. As I have indicated earlier, there are infrastructure areas which are absent. For example:

- what is Australia's national water strategy (beyond the Murray Darling)?
- what is Australia's national land management strategy?

The published thinking and national debate on those major issues is limited. Surely, we can do better. Governments and leadership in Australia need to address the big issues and questions about:

- Australia's place in the world and our national identity
- what industries will drive prosperity over the next 50 years
- building on our competitive advantages and resolving our competitive disadvantages
- identifying areas where we need to develop global competitive advantages
- measures of prosperity that we should be focusing on.

There is little new here. They are basic strategic questions any business needs to address. These questions can be broken down into three simple questions:

1. where are we now? (our current position)
2. where do we want to be? (our future position– our vision)
3. how will we measure our progress?

To avoid questions like these is to doom Australia to mediocrity. Businesses can't afford to ignore these questions and nor can government.

In addition, a major question in any strategic process is the issue of money – how do we allocate the resources? Ultimately this is a function of a successful business sector. The primary role of governments is to provide coherent policy continuity and support. Its source of funds is its taxing power, and no one wants to pay more tax. The challenge for governments is the same as the one facing every family/household – there are always more spending needs than money available. If we want to continue our prosperous lifestyle, something has to change. It's not a new idea, but if we focused on increasing the size of the pie it might help. To do that requires a focus on future industries and businesses.

Australia in the Global Context

Australia is historically and currently a prosperous country by any standards. But can we provide evidence that this prosperity will continue? Australia has a robust and vibrant business system, but the indicators are that we are a mid-range (mediocre) player in the global context.

The Legatum Prosperity Index is published each year and currently Australia ranks 13th overall on the following prosperity indicators:

- Economic Quality
- Business Environment
- Governance
- Education
- Health
- Safety & Security
- Personal Freedom
- Social Capital
- Natural Environment.[138]

138 https://infrastructureaustralia.gov.au/policy-publications/publications/Australian-Infrastructure-Plan.aspx

The fact is that we're also the 13th largest economy in the world.[139] So while we may not have the biggest market to exploit, we do have an economic platform of substance.

Indicators which are a possibility for measuring "Economic Quality" into the future are:

1. the number of 'for-profit' businesses started as a product of R&D investment, and
2. the number of people employed in those businesses.

Australia's Most Profitable Industries

The most recent statistics available indicate that Australia's most profitable industries are:

- administration and supply services
- mining
- retail
- hospitality
- and wholesale.[140]

These industries are a platform for the future. Innovation in these industries is therefore vital for our national future.

We also need to ask ourselves whether there are other industries currently travelling below the radar, which need increased innovation focus and support.

Australia's Globally Significant Industries

Australia's most globally significant industries in terms of our world rankings are provided below:[141]

- mining resources (top 3 in the world)
- tertiary education of foreign students (3rd largest in the world)

139 https://www.investopedia.com/insights/worlds-top-economies/
140 https://www.icas.com/ca-today-news/five-most-profitable-industries-in-australia
141 https://www.austrade.gov.au/international/invest/resources/benchmark-report-2018/charts/charts

- investment fund assets (6th largest in the world)
- international tourism receipts (10th largest in the world)
- agricultural products (top 12 in the world).

It is interesting to reflect that there is very little 'high value-adding' industry in Australia in physiology or medicine, despite the fact that we have had serious success over many years in terms of innovating in this area. Did you know that 7 of Australia's 11 Nobel Prize winners have been in physiology or medicine?[142] It's not a subject which receives much coverage, but it's a great record of success on which we can build. (For the record, all of Australia's Nobel Prize Winners are listed in the Appendix of this book).

The current value created in the healthcare industry is measured at a very high level by overall better health in the community, reduced expenditure in healthcare and increased productivity.

The biotechnology industry is recognised globally as being in the top 5 in the world and it employs 48,000 people.[143]

It is an industry of the future and one where STEM skills are highly sought. It is an emerging success story. As mentioned earlier in this book, we have CSL (a public company that was formerly a government entity), Cochlear and ResMed as globally recognised businesses in the healthcare industry.

How many of our other industries have businesses recognised globally? (I refer back to the Gardasil story – it could not be fully commercialised in Australia.)

Here is another example of a missed Australian commercialisation opportunity. A colleague of mine has recently had heart surgery to replace an aortic valve. He shared the following story with me:[144]

"Some aortic valve replacements are mechanical, some are from pigs, some are from cows, but very few (if any) are from people.

142 https://www.austrade.gov.au/international/invest/resources/benchmark-report-2018/charts/charts
143 https://www.ausbiotech.org/biotechnology-industry/fast-facts
144 Ron Carr – personal correspondence

Mine is from a cow. My cardiac surgeon told me that there are herds of donor cows bred for the purpose. The nearest herd is just north of Brisbane. The cows are taken to a local abattoir to be killed and the hearts are harvested. The hearts (or perhaps just parts of the hearts) are then flown to Singapore. I don't suppose the price is very high at that stage, probably better than cat food prices given the extra care in breeding and caring.

The factory or laboratory where the valves are made ready for use in patients had very specific requirements. The Singapore government stepped in and supplied what was needed, specifically:

- *a very green clean location with no dirty land uses nearby and*
- *a guaranteed uninterrupted electricity supply.*

A very favourable tax arrangement was also struck (perhaps none), whether or not that was also needed I don't know.

The workers are not all from Singapore, some come in daily from Malaysia. They are extraordinarily proud of their work and appreciate that the market acceptance of their high-value product could be lost in a moment of inattention.

Australia then buys the valves back at $25,000 each. We must buy lots of them because everyone knows one or two people getting about with a cow valve, they are good for 15 years or so. Kevin Rudd is on his second one. The Singapore factory supplies 80% of the world market."

Key Points

- Australia's most profitable industries are currently in administration and supply services, mining, retail, hospitality, and wholesale.
- Australia's most globally significant industries are mining, the tertiary education of foreign students, investment fund assets, international tourism, and agricultural products.
- Our biotechnology industry is ranked 5th in the world and it employs 48,000 people, yet the heart valves of cows grown and slaughtered in South Queensland are sold to the Singapore biotech sector to be transformed into heart valves for humans in Australia.

Chapter 8

CHANGE AND TRANSITION

"A noble purpose inspires sacrifice, stimulates innovation and encourages perseverance."

— Gary Hamel [145]

Introduction

This chapter focuses on change and transition. Transition is the process of adapting to change. Australia must confront and address multiple challenges to become a prosperous nation in the mid-to-late 21st century. Business needs to lead this conversation.

As I've mentioned earlier in this book, people tend to naturally crave certainty, stability, predictability and comfort. When this is disrupted (with change), a psychological process occurs whether we like it or not. You might note that when there are major incidents in schools and workplaces now, there are some who need counselling to help them adjust to the new reality.

In a work environment, change can include structural changes, technology changes, a change in strategy, new products, new leadership, or people changing jobs or employers (whether encouraged or by choice). At a broader level, the Australian economy has changed radically, and this change will accelerate. For example:

- global commodity prices have fallen and the 'mining boom' is over. The demand for our resources from China has dropped off.[146]
- the middle class in Australia is reducing in number.[147]
- the 'gig economy' is emerging.
- there is a focus on start-ups that we haven't seen before.

---

145 https://www.toolshero.com/toolsheroes/gary-hamel/

146 https://www.smh.com.au/business/the-economy/2018-the-end-of-the-resources-boom-as-falling-commodity-prices-bite-20180107-p4yyaa.html

147 https://www.smh.com.au/national/rising-inequality-is-hollowing-out-the-australian-middle-class-20181120-p50h2o.html

- globally, the changes created by technology (like robotics, artificial intelligence, 'big data' and genomics) have accelerated. New industries are emerging.

These are just a few of the issues that are affecting the Australian and global economies.

At the same time, there's also a movement to self-interest and self-protection (e.g. Brexit). Leaders like Donald Trump have also emerged, promising to return things to the way they were ('Make America Great Again'). That's resistance to change in action. It appears to me that Pauline Hanson (version 1) was an early symbol of the resistance to change in Australia.

It is fair to say that there are radical changes and disruptions in our current era, much of it caused by new technologies. Managing change is a life skill where it seems that many need help. Having worked professionally in this area for 40 years, one transition model which I have found useful is the work of William Bridges.[148] His work provides a framework and some language which have always helped me in understanding the issues to do with change and transition. I can say confidently that clients have found it helpful.

Three Stages of Transition

Transition is a psychological process that involves three stages. Let me explain.

Stage 1: letting go

This stage starts with an ending of the current status quo. The process of 'letting go' involves leaving or saying goodbye to old identities and/or old realities. There's an old baseball saying that's appropriate for this stage: '*You can't steal second base with your foot on first*'. This stage is often characterised by resistance and a range of behaviours and emotions which might include:

- leaving old identities and realities
- fear/anxiety
- denial

148 https://www.goodreads.com/book/show/159614.Managing_Transitions

- sadness
- a sense of loss.

Stage 2: the neutral phase

This stage begins with the realisation that transition must happen and that there are possibilities of renewal. But that realisation can also be accompanied by uncertainty and confusion over exactly what to do. It's not uncommon for people, organisations, governments and countries to feel like they're in 'no man's land' during this time.

This period of emotional wilderness is a dark time. People are still attached to the old idea or way and struggle to move forward. The experience might include:

- feelings of resentment
- a loss of meaning and therefore interest
- the (often tentative) search for something new
- the seeds of the future emerging.

Stage 3: the new beginnings

This is the stage where progress starts to be made. There is a sense of moving forward with accompanying behaviour changes. People, organisations, governments and countries can see a positive future. This phase is characterised by:

- a sense of excitement
- a step forward
- new learnings and behaviours.

All three transition stages are very human processes and each person experiences them uniquely. While having an awareness of them is important, it does not change the actual experience. Over the years, clients have said things like:

"I guess for everyone the pain is the pain, and we are all different."

"When I was in that 'no man's land' phase I thought I was the only one feeling like that – now I know I am normal."

"I did not know there were ways to explain this – it will make my job a bit easier."

Being able to verbalise the journey is an important part of the process and having a language system and a mind map to explain it makes it a lot easier.

The Importance of Foresight

The role of leadership in a time of great change (like we're experiencing right now) is to nurture the spirit of the system and to create hope. Leaders need to create a collective sense that 'we are creating a new future based in the 21st century'. Hope is the virtue that helps create the future.

A major role that government could play is to encourage the general population to think about and participate in an informed conversation about the future. Rather than focusing on the fear-based debate that has been a feature of our national conversations in recent years, there's the opportunity to create a conversation based on hope.

For example, there has been little conversation about the flow-on industry opportunities that might be created by:

- the government's $50 billion investment in expanding Australia's naval defence fleet via the Future Submarines program.[149] It could be argued that Apple would not be the business it is today without some of the technologies developed as part of the US Defence research in the 1960s and 1970s.
- the development of the Melbourne to Brisbane Inland Rail system.[150]
- the government's recent commitment to developing a space industry.[151]

There are many conceivable possibilities in the near and longer-term future, that up until recently would have been dismissed as 'pie in the sky'. For example:

- driverless cars

149 https://www.defencesa.com/projects/future-submarines
150 https://www.inlandrail.gov.au/
151 https://australianaviation.com.au/2019/03/adelaide-getting-two-new-space-facilities/

- drone delivery systems for food
- whole business systems being managed by robots, artificial intelligence and big data
- space travel.

And who would have thought that computer gaming would become a global 'sport'? There are now professional 'Esports' leagues and teams, along with national and international tournaments with serious prize money. The big teams are run like businesses and they have owners, CEOs, COOs, marketing/PR staff and sponsors. Team owners poach players just like they do in the real sporting world.

There is a whole generation who are growing up with these gaming/technology skills, which are the basis of future work and business. Other industries will emerge using this technology. Robotics, artificial intelligence, and data analytics will be the standard for the next generation. Their jobs will often involve working in 'control centres', managing robots and other technologies.

Recently, my daughter rang from the US to announce that her 11 year old son was in a robotics team competing in the State Robotics Championships. Naturally we were very excited. His team finished in the top two and so off to Louisville Kentucky they went (along with 30,000 others) to attend the World Robotics Championships. There were teams in every age group. One of my daughter's comments about it has stayed with me – *"Who would have thought I would have a son, who at 11 can skillfully design, build and drive a robot?"*

The future of the world is in the imaginations of the younger generations who are growing up in this technological world. How are their imaginations forming by using technology? That question is both wonderfully exciting and a little scary.

We simply can't afford to ignore the changes that are happening. But it requires imagination, courage and a commitment to a long-term perspective that an annual report or the three-year election cycle doesn't encourage.

Strategic Innovation

The capacity to be strategic usually doesn't come easily during times of change. There is a quote which captures this challenge perfectly: *"When you are up to your 'a-se' in alligators, it's really hard to remember that the objective is to drain the swamp."* (Anonymous).

Many business leaders often become so immersed in running their organisations that they struggle to develop the capacity to work and/or think strategically. (It's the same for political leaders.) The political system is designed to cripple the imagination and the emotional system. Thinking strategically and focusing on a big picture is the real challenge. In business, the focus on shareholder value is just as crippling.

At the heart of strategy development is having a conversation about whether it's possible to create the future. The alternative is to allow external forces to dictate and influence your future. In other words, to be reactive.

It appears there are countries which are leading the charge:

- Israel – the 'start-up nation'
- China – with its Belt Road Initiative (explained in more detail in Chapter 10) and many others
- South Korea –with companies like Samsung, Hyundai, LG and Kia Motors
- Singapore – it is attracting investments in biotechnology and pharmaceuticals, aerospace, electronics, and other advanced industries like clean technology. Apple, Microsoft, Bosch, Novartis and many other companies have their regional headquarters in Singapore
- Scandinavian countries.

And Australia? 'Relaxed and comfortable' – committed to lifestyle. When was the last time in Australia we had a real conversation based on hope and potential? Business can lead this conversation. We need to lift our game.

There are three basic questions that any business must answer to start developing an effective strategy. They are:

1. where are we now? (our current position)
2. where do we want to be? (our future position)

3. how will we get there? (the stages/steps to get there)

The questions are the same for a nation – just harder to grapple with. It's what our political process is supposed to do.

There are also a number of tougher (existential) questions that need to be answered as part of strategy development. They challenge our very existence and in Australia they really are questions about:

- our identity – who are we?
- our values – what do we stand for?
- our position in the world – what is our strategic position?
- what is our 'prosperity template' for 2050?
- what is our future in a rapidly changing world?

These are difficult questions to answer and it takes time to build a shared understanding. Many business leaders pay lip service to them by focusing on profitability, return on investment, and shareholder value. While shareholder value is important, it is not the core purpose of business. It is a very limited and self-interested perspective. It requires little intellectual or emotional effort. Any organisation that doesn't answer the big questions in some way is soulless and rudderless. It will struggle to survive in today's rapidly changing environment.

Business leadership is really about helping an organisation to address these questions so that its customers, employees, suppliers, shareholders and the community all experience the benefits in terms of prosperity. The self-serving approach we have seen from some of our large banks in recent years is symbolic of a business culture which in many ways has lost sight of the purpose of business. We need a robust, vibrant and ethical business sector for Australia to be a prosperous nation. It is the only way we can all enjoy a high standard of living and have a great lifestyle. For Australia to be a country that is fair and just with a safety net that protects the less fortunate, there is no option.

If Australia is to play any role in the world in the future – it will be much better to have strategies for our nation (articulated as a coherent set of economic and social directions), rather than for us to be a part of some other nation's strategy.

The role of leadership at every level is to feed the soul of businesses and communities by creating a positive narrative about the future. One way of doing this is to work to address tough questions with the community.

Business with Purpose

Jennifer Westacott (the CEO of the Business Council of Australia) has lamented the lack of business focus on purpose:

"I'm not convinced that enough of our organisations have got a genuine focus on purpose.

I'm not sure they constantly ask the question – why?

Yes, many have well-crafted mission statements. But that is not the same as a true understanding of the 'why' – a clarity of direction that is shared across the organisation."[152]

The comments by Westacott are provocative. If leaders in Australia had a genuine purpose beyond making money how would they behave? Maybe there would be more and better leaders to help us capitalise on new opportunities in a rapidly changing world. They could engage in a more strategic conversation about the big issues identified by the CSIRO documents that I've referred to in Chapter 9 of this book.

Over the years I've facilitated thousands of strategy workshops in hundreds of organisations and businesses. When it comes to identifying their business purpose, I challenge the business leaders in these sessions by telling them 'the stonemason story' that I first heard many years ago.

Three stonemasons in the middle ages were hard at work when a visitor came along and asked them what they were doing.

–The first stonemason was hard at work, sweat on his brow.

"I am cutting this stone", he grumbled.

–The second stone mason, though less distraught, responded with a deep sigh,

152 www.theaustralian.com.au/news/inquirer/lets-make-it-our-business-to-become-a-nation-with-purpose/news-story/54384d18ac39e32687ca7e2092624637

"I'm building a parapet".

–The third stonemason replied with a radiant face,

"I am building a beautiful cathedral that will glorify God for centuries to come".

Sometimes it is matter of perspective. The human spirit yearns to be part of something greater, to make a difference. By definition it is aspirational. The core purpose of a business is the animating force that can be a source of passion and the reason people get out of bed to go to work in the morning. If enough businesses focused on understanding their purpose (beyond just making money) and then acted accordingly, Australia is potentially a nation with a much greater purpose.

Over the next 50 years the role of business and business leadership is crucial to our prosperity.

Key Points

- Change and transition are different concepts. Transition is the process of adapting to change.
- There are three stages of transition.
- There are countries leading the charge to 'create the future'.
- Having a purpose is important for both people and businesses.

PART FOUR

A New Australian Narrative for the Future

Chapter 9
THE INNOVATION CONTEXT

"Someone has to invest in creating the movies of the future."

—Eric Fellner[153]

Introduction

This chapter outlines the major global trends that will impact Australia in the future.

The innovation debate in Australia has had a very limited context – it has been a conversation in a vacuum. How does anyone make sense of it? For innovation to have any meaning, the context has to be robust.

In Chapter 4 I highlighted that in business there is a focus on:

- work system innovation
- product innovation and
- business model innovation.

If we take a broader view, we must include social policy innovation and cultural innovation. Remember Australia was considered to be a pioneer in many areas – a social experiment. Building on this story is an important part of our future. In a world which might be described as socially dislocated, new models and technologies are important.

In 2012, the CSIRO produced a seminal report titled *Our Future World: Global megatrends that will change the way we live.*[154] It should be compulsory reading for all business leaders (if not all Australians). The report creates a context for some of the big conversations that Australian business must have sooner rather than later. It provides an opportunity for conversation focusing on the future and the big questions, rather than the 'here and now' problems.

The report predicted that the following megatrends will have a major impact on Australia over the next twenty years:

---

153 https://www.brainyquote.com/quotes/eric_fellner_646781

154 https://www.csiro.au/en/Do-business/Futures/Reports/Our-Future-World

More from less

The earth has limited supplies of natural mineral, energy, water and food resources essential for human survival and maintaining lifestyles.

Going, going, ... gone?

Many of the world's natural habitats, plant species and animal species are in decline and/or at risk of extinction.

The silk highway

Coming decades will see the world economy shift from west to east and north to south.

Forever young

The ageing population is an asset. Australia and many other countries that make up the Organisation for Economic Cooperation and Development (OECD) have an ageing population.

Virtually here

This megatrend explores what might happen in a world of increased connectivity where individuals, communities, governments and businesses are immersed in the virtual world to a much greater extent than ever before.

Great expectations

This is a consumer, societal, demographic and cultural megatrend. It explores the rising demand for experiences over products and the rising importance of social relationships.

The Seventh Megatrend – the Innovation Imperative

In 2015, the CSIRO's Stefan Hajkowicz identified *'the innovation imperative'* as the seventh megatrend in his book *Global Megatrends: Seven Patterns of Change Shaping Our Future*. He described the innovation imperative as follows: *"The last megatrend is about accelerating technological advancement and the importance of innovation... we explore the rise of regenerative medicine which could keep human beings living for hundreds of years. We explore advances in energy storage systems (batteries) which could revolutionise the way we power our cities, our cars, our planes and the whole economy... Overall, this megatrend points towards a world where human innovation makes (just about) anything possible."*[155]

Australia's Response to the Megatrends

The big question for business (and dare I say Australia) is:

How do we respond to these megatrends in a way that creates sustainable national prosperity and development?

In other words, how do we leverage our assets and competence to create wealth and prosperity for Australia's future to grow the wealth creation pie? Wealth creation is the platform for prosperity.

There can be no genuine strategic conversation without an understanding of these megatrends. Successful businesses are in a continuing conversation about them so that they can develop strategies and make decisions in the right context.

Australia needs to have a more widespread and serious debate about what kind of industries we want for the future of this country. Where is the prosperity going to come from in the next fifty years? How do we position Australia to address these trends, so Australia is better prepared for the business environment of the future? The context for any debate on reform or transition must focus on potential growth industries, rather than those that are in an inevitable decline. National prosperity comes from a high-performing business sector.

I have no doubt there are many talented people in Australia doing work on these megatrends and developing policy. Certainly, in recent years numerous reports have been published, but my question when we look at the debate in Australia – both in business and in government, is – what are we talking about? And who is doing the talking? The megatrends identified in the CSIRO report are influencing our future now, but they seem to be a long way from anyone's awareness in the public debate.

Business leadership requires an understanding of Australia's global context. Building this strategic competence is a real priority for leaders so that they can think imaginatively about the future and act courageously by identifying

155 https://www.publish.csiro.au/book/7265/

and capitalising on shifts, trends and discontinuities that are occurring globally in all industries and markets.

Once business leaders have developed a strategic context, they can lead informed conversations with their teams about a range of possible futures. These scenarios are likely to require at least some degree of innovation so that their organisations can not only survive but thrive in the future. Two factors in Australia's strategic context are our geographic location within Asia and the development of Northern Australia.

Australia and the Asian Context

I outlined in Chapter 1 of this book that British settlement of Australia in 1788 made our country an outpost of Britain. Our political and legal systems are British. Much of our early social fabric also emerged from Britain. This culture only started to dissipate during and post-World War II when our dependence moved towards the United States.

There is no doubt that Australia is now increasingly a 'Eurasian' nation. It is where we are located. We ignored this geographic reality for many years, and as a business nation we were slow to respond to the business opportunities on our proverbial doorstep. There are a number of reasons for that, including different languages, different cultures, and different ways of doing business.

But we now have a number of key free trade agreements in place. The potential implications of Australian businesses focusing on Asia are huge and positive. I must admit, I find it surprising that an Asian language is not compulsory in our education system from K-12. Instead, we still cling to French and German.

The Australian government published the *Australia in the Asian Century* white paper in 2012. This is a fairly general document, but there is one clear objective in terms of trade:

Australia's trade links with Asia will be at least one-third of GDP by 2025, up from one quarter in 2011.[156]

156 http://www.defence.gov.au/whitepaper/2013/docs/australia_in_the_asian_century_white_paper.pdf

Northern Australia

In 2015, the federal government published the *Our North, Our Future* white paper on developing Northern Australia.[157] This paper was written in the following context:

- the economies of South East Asia and southern China are within three to five flying hours from Darwin.
- the Tropics (i.e. areas that are geographically in the middle of the globe, including parts of Asia, Australia, Africa, North and South America) account for 40 per cent of the world's population, and are predicted to account for 50 per cent by 2050.
- Asia is predicted to have about two-thirds of the global middle-class population by 2030.
- the north operates in similar time zones to the most dynamic economies in Asia. This is a particular advantage for service industries.
- Australia had recently concluded free trade agreements (FTAs) with Japan, South Korea and China.
- the region is seen as a gateway for Australia's defence and security operations.

Some serious targets for 2030 were proposed in the paper, including the following:

- Doubling Australia's agricultural output by developing a food bowl that includes premium produce.
- Growing the tourist economy in the north of Australia to two million international tourists annually.
- Building an energy export industry worth $150 billion to the Australian economy, with a major focus on clean and efficient energy.

This focus on the development of Northern Australia and its possible substantial relationship with Asia is another small step on Australia's future journey. The platform that industries need to grapple with is the concept of

157 https://www.industry.gov.au/data-and-publications/our-north-our-future-white-paper-on-developing-northern-australia

actually establishing longer-term objectives. This is a challenging process and it needs serious support from both industry and the community.

Asia consists of multiple countries and markets, each with separate and discrete needs and wants, as well as profoundly different cultures. The change in thinking required for Australia to embrace this opportunity is huge. The first step is to accept Australia as an independent 'Eurasian nation'. This is crucial, because the Asia-Pacific region is forecast to be bigger in terms of economic output than all the Western nations combined by 2024.[158]

Key Points

- In 2012, the CSIRO produced a seminal report titled *Our Future World: Global megatrends that will change the way we live.*
- In 2015, the CSIRO's Stefan Hajkowicz identified "the innovation imperative" as the seventh megatrend in his book *Global Megatrends: Seven Patterns of Change Shaping Our Future.*
- In 2015, the federal government published the *Our North, Our Future* white paper on developing Northern Australia.
- Asia is predicted to have about two-thirds of the global middle-class population by 2030.

158 Phil Ruthven – IBISWorld Where Knowledge is Power, May 2014

Chapter 10

A NEW AUSTRALIAN NARRATIVE – MOON SHOTS

"The sky is not the limit...there are footprints on the Moon."

—Buzz Aldrin[159]

Introduction

For Australia to be a truly innovative nation, we need to have national conversations that lead and encourage people to aspire to great things. In this time of massive global disruption, we must create a national story which will unite Australians and allow us to see a future filled with hope (not fear).

Australian leaders have an opportunity to focus the energy of the nation. Wouldn't it be great if each year the leaders of the country could come together and announce a 'moon shot'? In Chapter 3, I defined a 'moon shot' as follows:

- *A transformative nation-building project with a 30-50-year timeframe that has bipartisan support and focuses on:*
- *developing our contribution to humanity, and/or*
- *building major physical infrastructure that creates (or provides a vehicle for the creation of) national prosperity.*

In short, 'moon shots' refer to aspirational goals. It's a nod to the achievement of one of the most aspirational goals in history, the US landing a man on the Moon. It was a goal that galvanised an entire nation, and arguably the world. In this chapter, I propose some potential 'moon shots' for Australia.

China is an example of a country with 'moon shots.' Consider the Belt Road Initiative. This project commenced in 2013 with the aim of linking China with Central and South Asia, North Africa and onward toward Europe. In all, 65 countries are involved. These countries collectively account for over

159 https://twitter.com/therealbuzz/status/1022431200340860928

30% of global GDP, 62% of the population and 75% of the known energy reserves.[160]

This is a project of huge global consequence and yet we hear very little about it in Australia. China is an example of a country with a long-term view. In fact, when Australia recently leased the Darwin port to the Chinese for 99 years, we were arguably becoming a part of the Chinese strategy.[161] Or does it mean we have a 99-year strategy for Northern Australia that few know about? More likely it is a 'thought bubble' or knee-jerk response by a small group of 'leaders' who could see the possibility of a quick buck and who have no concept of strategy. My question is where does China fit into Australia's long-term (100-year) strategy?

In addition to the Belt Road Initiative, China has also been working on the following projects for at least a decade:[162]

- building a network of ultramodern airports
- building a web of high-speed trains connecting its major cities
- launching their own stem cell/genetic engineering industry and
- creating an electric car industry, starting in 20 pilot cities.

Here's a literal 'moon shot' that China has also achieved. Early in 2019, they managed to land a spacecraft on the far side of the Moon, where no human or robot has ever ventured before.[163] And as I mentioned earlier in the book, Israel recently launched their first space mission to the Moon.[164] It only took them just over 8 years.

Australia was once a leader in space research. We opted out of the space race only to re-join it in recent years. Maybe a real Moon shot within 7 years is a realistic Australian target?

160 https://www.worldbank.org/en/topic/regional-integration/brief/belt-and-road-initiative
161 https://www.abc.net.au/news/2019-03-12/why-did-northern-territory-sell-darwin-port-to-china-what-risk/10755720
162 http://www.nytimes.com/2010/09/26/opinion/26friedman.html?_r=0
163 https://www.nationalgeographic.com.au/science/china-just-landed-on-the-far-side-of-the-moon-what-comes-next.aspx
164 https://www.space.com/spacex-israeli-moon-lander-satellites-launch-success.html

Ten 'Moon Shot' Ideas for Australia

Creating our future requires a level of thinking which is uncommon in our culture. Below I've tried to visually capture the key elements that should be used to inform our 'moon shots'.

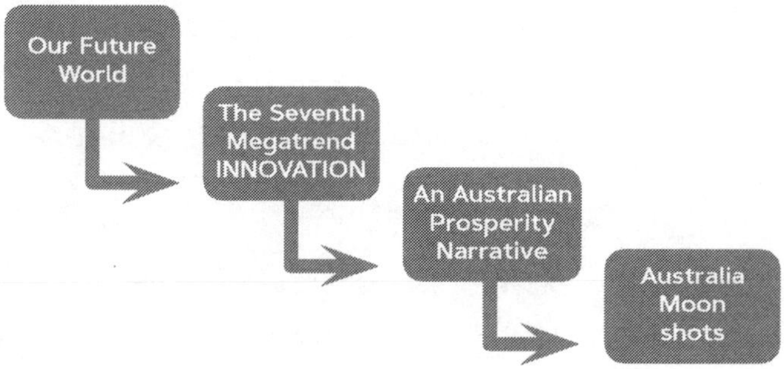

Using this model as a guide, below are some 'moon shot' ideas, in no particular order.

Many of these have been articulated in other places and I'm confident there are greater minds than mine with more perspective who could refine, prioritise or even create a new, more dynamic and robust list. I hope so. Here goes:

1. **Australia: the healthiest nation in the world – leading the world in all health-related areas.**

   No surprise here. (This is an opportunity identified in the Australia 2030: Prosperity through Innovation report).

2. **Biotechnology to replace mining as a major driver of Australia's wealth creation**

   There are multiple possibilities for exploration within this sector, like 'MedTech', 'FoodTech' and 'CleanTech'. Current data indicates that we are a leader in these technologies, with 500 'MedTech', 350 'EdTech', and 300 'FoodTech' companies.[165]

3. **An Australian Nestlé (a global top 5 food / fibre brand)**

   In a world of nine billion people, food and fibre are central to the future. There is evidence that many overseas countries see

165 2018 Benchmark Australia Report, p. 14.

huge value in owning Australian food and fibre companies. It does strike me as strange that all these investors can see more value in our food and fibre businesses than we can. Why are most of the food brands in Australian supermarkets owned by international companies?

4. **A national transport system modelled on the best in the world**

   This could be done by developing major transport hubs in Toowoomba, Townsville, Darwin and The Pilbara and using them as 'gateways to Asia', our major future markets. The Wagner family in Toowoomba have established a benchmark.

   It would require the development of world-class road, rail and air systems in these regions to facilitate fast and efficient distribution. For example, a high-speed rail network connecting regional areas with capital cities. It appears there are embryonic conversations occurring in the ether now.[166] *(However, a sobering thought is that it's taken 30 years for the Melbourne to Brisbane Rail system stage to get traction.)*

5. **Australia as a renewable energy hub for the world (especially for Asian countries)**

   This could be achieved by exporting renewable energy from north-western Australia to dramatically cut energy poverty for hundreds of millions in Asia.[167]

   Australia has abundant natural resources – coal, gas, sun and uranium – but it appears we do not think either big enough or beyond ourselves. Instead of having a debate about how dangerous coal is, we could be debating about how we can build our clean energy capabilities and use our resources to make a difference in the lives of those who have little energy.

6. **Australia is water resilient for a population of 70-100 million**

   This would require a major water project (or projects) being undertaken for Northern and Central Australia so that we become water abundant. Can anyone remember the last substantial water project in Australia?

---

166 https://www.abc.net.au/news/2019-03-11/is-high-speed-fast-rail-in-australian-cities-possible/10876046

167 https://theconversation.com/the-norths-future-is-electrifying-powering-asia-with-renewables-17286

Snowy 2.0 has recently commenced, but it's a drop in the ocean. The Murray Darling? This may well be a project with major benefits, but it appears there are big questions about it.[168]

We could learn from the South-to-North Water Diversion Project in China. China's four main rivers are currently being linked via three diversion routes that will be constructed over the next 50-year time frame. The planned completion date is 2050, when an estimated 44.8 billion cubic metres of water will be able to be diverted annually to the population centres in the drier north regions of China.[169] *Why isn't something similar being done in Australia?*

7. **Australia in the Top 10 defence technology exporters in the world**

   This ties in with Australia's recently increased commitment to defence technologies and related industries.[170]

8. **The resurrection of Australia's manufacturing sector (via Advanced Manufacturing) to approach 15% of our gross value-added product**

   Advanced Manufacturing is one of the federal government's six identified six growth centres, as outlined in Chapter 6. If we are to have any chance of commercialising our national research, our manufacturing base needs to be increased.

9. **Australia's trade links with Asia to be at least 50% by 2050**

   We need to position Australia so that our geographic position is a competitive advantage. Key elements are likely to include our:

   - connectivity
   - physical infrastructure (ports, airports and land transport systems)
   - stable institutions and robust economy.

10. **An Australian space project – landing a person on the Moon**

    In most industries there are indicative measures which are obvious. In space, it is hard to beat 'landing a person on the Moon'. It worked for the

168 https://www.abc.net.au/radio/programs/am/investigation-reveals-murray-darling-basin-plan-deeply-flawed/11287058

169 https://www.water-technology.net/projects/south_north/western parts of the country.

170 https://www.business.gov.au/centre-for-defence-industry-capability/defence-innovation/defence-innovation-hub

US in the 1960s – why not for Australia again? It sure beats gold medals at the Olympics. It might be a moon shot which would galvanise Australians?

At a national level, Australia now has a commitment to the development of space technology. Globally, the space economy is valued at US$345 billion. Australia's share of that pie is $3.9 billion, with 10,000 people employed in the sector. The majority of those are in the commercial sector. The goal is to grow those numbers to $12 billion and 30,000 employees respectively by 2030.[171]

Any of these projects have the potential to make a huge difference to the lives of Australians and the Australian economy. I am confident many others could be named and discussed.

Australia has a robust economy and we need to value it and build on it. This will depend on business and government working together to create a new future. As mentioned earlier in this book, we are the world's 13th largest economy in our 28th continuous year of economic growth. This is an extraordinary phenomenon.

We also have low government debt and we are geographically positioned in Asia with strong relationships. For example, we recently signed a free trade agreement with Indonesia and already have existing agreements in place with China, Japan, Korea, Malaysia, Thailand and Singapore.[172] There will be huge growth in Asia over the next 50 years.

We are a diversified service-based economy. Our services and technology sectors have great potential, and our productivity is globally competitive in many sectors. But there is no reason for complacency.

Our predisposition for recreation and lifestyle is a great advantage, but it is also a major risk.

There is a risk we are becoming the 'lifestyle trash' of Asia.[173] Treasurer Paul Keating alluded to this 25 years ago. If we don't have strategic vision and some pathways to achieve them, we might be remembered as a nation that was once prosperous (with 28 consecutive years of economic growth) but finished up being a 'branch office nation' (we are now), employing 'the

171 https://www.createdigital.org.au/australia-global-hub-space-tourism/
172 https://dfat.gov.au/trade/agreements/pages/trade-agreements.aspx
173 https://theconversation.com/revisiting-the-banana-republic-and-other-familiar-destinations-15088

serfs of Asia.' Note that there are poor nations in the world today that were once wealthy.

The world is not standing still – there are countries in Asia and Africa driven by more urgent imperatives than we face. These countries will own the future if we don't embrace the opportunities it offers. We will be remembered as a settler economy that peaked and faded.

Innovation is crucial to Australia navigating our future. There are a number of trends and opportunities that we can potentially exploit in emerging and existing industries. Australian business needs to be at the forefront of this debate, driving Australia's wealth creation and prosperity. Both business and government need to display a form of thought leadership which is uncommon (dare I say absent) in the last 20 years.

Innovation requires:

- imagination
- foresight
- courage
- competence
- resilience
- and dare I say it, some mongrel.

Without these attributes, our pursuit of the relaxed and comfortable lifestyle will overwhelm us.

Key Points

- In this time of huge global disruption, we must create a national story (including moon shots) which will unite Australians.
- Australia has a robust economy and we need to value it and build on it. Otherwise, we will be left behind other countries who are seizing new opportunities.
- Innovation is crucial to Australia navigating our future.

CONCLUSION

In my journey writing this book I have discovered and highlighted a number of issues facing Australia right now in a rapidly changing and globalised world. How we respond will have a significant impact on the prosperity of future generations of Australians. We simply can't afford to stick our heads in the sand with a typical Australian 'she'll be right' attitude.

I've also highlighted that business must play a key role in creating Australia's future wealth. Prosperity does not occur without a robust business environment and visionary, courageous leadership. Significantly though, the following question was asked in a 2019 survey of business leaders: *How prepared is your organisation for future trends?*

Their answers were a little scary:

- 7% not at all
- 34% moderately
- 46% satisfactorily
- 11% well
- 1% extremely well.[174]

Need I say any more? (Mediocrity wins again.)

I've also talked about the importance of vision-driven ('big picture') planning. That requires us to consider how we see Australia evolving over the next 50 years: Is Australia:

- an intellectual property hub (where our intellectual property is generally licensed or sold offshore)?
- a business incubator (where any business of substance is sold to the highest bidder)?

OR

- a business leader in some value-added industries, capitalising on the billions we have spent on R&D over so many years?

174 AGS 2019 Survey, published in *Company Director* April 2019, p.19

- a nation that has transformed itself from a service economy to a serious, high- technology industry hub for Asia and the world?

Building industries based on Australian innovation is the way to increase the size of the pie to ensure Australia's future prosperity. It requires a shift of mind at every level of Australian business and government. It will also require some radically different approaches. It will require a form of business and government leadership which we have not seen in recent years, if ever. The nature of business conversation will have to change. Here are some initiatives that could contribute to the 'mind shift' required.

1. **A Prosperity (Royal) Commission (every 10 years)**

   Earlier, I suggested convening a Prosperity (Royal) Commission to address issues of national significance focusing on Australia in 2075. It is a radical thought to use a 'problem-solving' mechanism like a Royal Commission to address a 'prosperity' topic. But recall the China Belt Road Initiative and South-to-North Water Diversion Project in China. Both of these projects have time frames for completion of more than 50 years. How can these sorts of long-term projects happen in Australia (or even be discussed)?

2. **The establishment of an independent (permanent) Prosperity Commission (to build on and extend) the work of the Royal Commission.**

   We were so disappointed after not winning a single gold medal at the 1976 Montreal Olympics that we actually did something about it. The Australian Sports Commission was established. Why not an Australian Prosperity Commission?

3. **An Australian Prosperity Report every three years**

   This Report could position Australia in a global context. Our current rankings leave the possibility of being better. The Report could be used as a platform for education and debate about our future policy development.

4. **Industry learning forums every three years**

   Business/industry/government could hold regular forums to educate and create a 'learning agenda' in each industry. There might even be debate and discussion about industry moon shots.

5. **An industry-business measurement system focusing on For-profit businesses established as a result of our R&D investment.**

   What if we measured the number of 'for-profit' businesses established (and the number of jobs created) as a result of national R&D investment?

6. **An innovation venture fund**

   This fund could be based on at least three sources:

   a) *a levy (tax) on every business transaction that involves an international investor buying an Australian business. (The purpose being the re-creation of Australian business.)*

   b) *dividends back to government from investments in government-funded R&D research which is later commercialised.*

   c) *the Business Council of Australia and other leading industry bodies contributing to this fund and working with government on prioritising a list of nation-building innovations that they believe Australia needs over the next 50 years.*

7. **Nation-building projects: bi-partisan agreement on infrastructure projects. One announced each parliamentary term.**

   Our infrastructure projects should never end up as political footballs like the NBN. Instead, the government and opposition should jointly announce at least one major nation-building project every election term.

If you don't like these, what are your ideas to shift the focus of the nation?

There will be some who read this book who believe that the real issues facing Australia are social justice and the development of world class education health and welfare system. It is hard to argue with those sentiments. The ultimate measure of a society includes how well we manage these issues. But I believe that if our wealth creation system (business) does not lift its game, specifically in terms of commercialising our intellectual property, then all of our current social systems are at risk.

In generations to come, our children's children will inevitably evaluate how our generation performed as nation-builders. Below are just a few of the questions they're likely to ask.

- Where are the great businesses built by Australians?
- Are there any Australian global brands?

- Where are the industries that exist because of the billions invested in Australian research?
- Why did Australia sell so much of its innovation internationally and who received the benefits?
- Did Australian businesses ever acquire businesses from other countries for the benefit of Australia?
- What major infrastructure was built for future generations?
- Did Australia allow the economics of globalisation to subsume it?
- Why are we a 'branch office' country?
- How much of Australia's potential prosperity was sold off to international interests?
- Will anyone in the world be looking to Australia as a model for industry building and wealth creation in 2075?

Acknowledgements

In 2011 my daughter Philippa encouraged me to enter the social media world. A world so foreign it could have been Mars. But it is where my serious writing started. Blogging (writing) has been a long, at times disheartening journey with a few mountains and more valleys. In the search for a theme for my Blogging, the innovation debate fortuitously arrived. At the time I resurrected a copy of a report written in 1991 by an international consulting group. And no surprise, many of the issues were the same then as they are now. This was a starting point for me. What has happened since then? What are we really achieving? Where is the evidence? Who are the leaders? These were just some of the questions? Over 100 Blogs later I had the kernel of the book you are now reading. Many have contributed none more than the over 2000 plus business leaders I have worked with over many years. As they say, "it takes a tribe!"

Each business leader, each business has their own unique challenges. Being competitive in a volatile, uncertain, complex and ambiguous business environment is just one. It has ever been thus!

In the early blogs Shona Makin, my social media coach, not only showed me how to load Blogs and manage a web site – she was a great support as an external reviewer and motivator. A blog every week!

Over many years some colleagues have also challenged me to write about my experiences as a Management Consultant and mentor to business leaders over 40 years. That's another book!

To David Fagan and Damien Brennan who read collections of blogs and encouraged me to believe this could be a book.

I am so grateful to the many who have assisted me over the last few years but specifically the last 10 months:

To those who have painstakingly read drafts and who have provided hugely valuable written and oral feedback and very welcome support: Brad Sands, Euan Murdoch, Ron Carr, Dr Richard Miller, Pam Varcoe, Dermot Kehoe, Rachael Kehoe, Vern Harnish, Theo Psaros, Alex Ihlenfeldt.

To my children and their husbands and wives who have read it – and selectively have provided feedback. I am very grateful. You are all a continuing inspiration the way you are living your lives at the edge in a loving and adventurous way.

To my editor - there is no way this could have happened without John Coomer (Editor). He took a bundle of Blogs and gave them coherence and meaning- and then rewrote and reshaped my best efforts. I am very grateful. He mentioned some time ago that authors often clubbed their work to death. I have successfully done that John. I did not follow all your advice!

To Sandra Harding and John Wagner for very kindly reading the final draft and contributing a review. I am very grateful. To a former client now friend, colleague and co-conspirator Euan Murdoch – this is really a social experiment. For 30 years now we have explored the boundaries of learning in business. Writing a foreword is a learning curve for you; writing a book is a learning curve for me!

To Sally, my wife, my best friend, my dogged and persistent supporter, and an enduring editor. You are a talent beyond words. There is nothing you cannot do. Parenting partner, schoolteacher, business partner, art gallery director and general project manager (and personal coach). As it turns out you might have made a living as an editor. You are bloody good at it. Every sentence I have written over the years you have edited – hundreds of thousands of words.

Every day with you is a joy. As Ronald Reagan said about Nancy in a farewell speech at the Whitehouse:

"I am happier than any man is entitled to be because I married you!"

I could not have said it better!

To the many I hope will read this work – thank you – you have choices to make?

APPENDIX – AUSTRALIA'S NOBEL PRIZE WINNERS

Year	Name	Domain
1915	Sir William Henry Bragg and Professor William Lawrence Bragg	Physics
1945	Sir Howard Florey	Physiology or Medicine (penicillin)
1960	Sir Frank Macfarlane Burnet	Physiology or Medicine (immunology)
1963	Sir John Carew Eccles	Physiology or Medicine (nerve cells)
1970	Sir Bernard Katz	Physiology or Medicine (nerve physiology)
1973	Patrick White	Literature
1975	Professor John Cornforth	Chemistry
1996	Professor Peter Doherty	Physiology or Medicine (immunology)
2005	Doctor J. Robin Warren and Professor Barry Marshall	Physiology or Medicine (discovery of the bacterium that causes stomach ulcers and gastritis)
2009	Professor Elizabeth Blackburn	Physiology or Medicine (genetics)
2011	Professor Brian Schmidt	Physics

About the Author

Ben Kehoe has worked for four decades at the coal face of Australian business as a social pioneer, storyteller, change agent, management consultant and business owner. His real work is working with business leaders to "make stuff happen".

Working with the chairman, CEOs, and leadership teams, he focuses on the core questions an organisation must answer to address their potential with integrity. He works with them to address the real issues that stand in their way – prioritisation, accountability, resistance and fear.

His work supports leadership teams in creating the future: creating new markets, toppling big players, securing competitive advantage, managing high growth and boosting profitability. In all of this, the issue of innovation is paramount.

Ben is a husband, father and grandfather, a student of business and life, a jogger, skier, art collector and ballroom dancer. Over the last decade, he has been exploring social media and its impact on business and the world at large.

Made in the USA
Monee, IL
05 November 2026

67379460R20098